THE ADVISOR'S GUIDE TO BUSINESS WEALTH

THE MOST IMPORTANT BUSINESS DECISION YOUR CLIENT WILL EVER MAKE

DAVID WAYNE WIMER

First Edition

Although the author and publisher have made every effort to ensure that the information in this book was correct at press time, the author and publisher do not assume and hereby disclaim any liability to any party for any loss, damage, or disruption caused by errors or omissions, whether such errors or omissions result from negligence, accident, or any other cause.

This is a work of creative nonfiction. While all the events in this book occurred, certain circumstances are portrayed to the best of the author's memory. Specific names and identifying details have been omitted to protect the privacy of the people and companies involved.

Published by
Munn Avenue Press
300 Main Street, Ste 21
Madison, NJ 07940
MunnAvenuePress.com

Contact the Author:
T: 484-269-7700 E: author@davidwimer.com

Manufactured & Produced in the United States of America

Paperback ISBN: 979-8-9859815-2-0
eBook ISBN: 979-8-9859815-3-7

CONTENTS

Per Angusta ad Augusta
[Through Trials to Triumph]

This is dedicated to all advisors serving a business owner.
May you always shine as a guiding beacon of light,
as you navigate an ocean of complexity and chance events.
And may true value always be at your side.

David Wayne Wimer

PROLOGUE
WHY I WROTE THIS GUIDE

You may be a certified financial planner, wealth manager, registered investment advisor, M&A advisor, turnaround expert, financial consultant, or an internal advisor such as a Chief Financial Officer. In that light, you and I have complimentary roles—we provide financial insight and recommendations to business owners. We exist to serve clients by helping them with their decisions surrounding fiscal management.

This guide shares insights gleaned over a 40+ year career in business. It covers value, timing, risk, complexity, hidden chasms, value gaps, and protection against chance events. With all of that in mind, the single most important business decision your business owner clients will ever make is grounded in one question: to Value-Prep, or not to Value-Prep?

You may have heard of, studied, read about, or may even

have suggested a Fair Market Value (FMV) business valuation. It is a fundamental, point-in-time snapshot of the value the owner has been working to achieve to that date. Our focus isn't how to read, interpret or calculate the FMV of a business. That's left to expert, certified valuators. Our journey is more practical in nature and answers a key question: now that we have the valuation, what do we do with it? That is the focus of *The Advisor's Guide to Finding, Building & Protecting Business Wealth*: to find, build, and protect the true value of a business.

A FMV valuation is an essential stake in the ground. Yet it is only the first step in our value-prepping journey together. Most clients review the valuation calculation, agree or disagree with it, then move on and get back to work. For them, its usefulness is temporary. As a Value Advisor, we will soon see its evergreen utility. It is also where we begin our quest.

What do we mean by "true value"? Finding true value in a business is like setting out to find hidden treasure. Without a map would you expect to easily find it? Unless you are on the right path and understand exactly what you are looking for, you are just digging holes, hoping you find the right spot. Likewise, unless a client understands where their business' true value lies, when the time comes to make a strategic business decision to RENEW, BUILD, BUY OR SELL the business, they can miss or give away the valuable and oftentimes hidden treasure. With 70%+ of their personal wealth tied up and locked inside their business, this one measure has rare significance. Therefore, what your client does with their valuation is the first step in the true value process.

Fluency in the concept of true value will help you to be perceived as an elite advisor, making it easier to identify, attract, convert and retain new business owner clients for the life of your practice. If you are a CFO, you will better support and protect your owner's business and the business wealth locked inside it for the life of your career.

You will gain in a few days reading what took me a career to understand, codify into a proven process and now teach to fellow advisors. My hope is you will become proficient at discussing and guiding your business owner prospects and clients on finding, building and protecting the true value in their business. We describe these actions as "value-prepping" the business.

Your clients may choose to confront their state of business readiness, de-risk their business and armor it against chance events now. Or they may choose to ignore it. The choice to value-prep now has a low cost. It is *de minimis* compared to the excessive costs to salvage value after an unmitigated risk or chance event occurs. When value-prepping is confronted early in a business' life cycle, you may end up looking like a genius down the road, without ever having to do anything special. Your role is to educate and create awareness, leading a client to a tool that helps them execute their vision seamlessly and flawlessly.

We also have a companion book for business owners to read, *The Tale of Mac & Murphy: The Most Important Business Decision You Will Ever Make.* I wrote it to engage owners in the conversation of value-prepping benefits. Owners will decide if value-prepping is worthy of adoption. If the true value is buried treasure, then an owner follows our map to find it and we provide them the tools to dig for and protect it. With your support, more owners will see the longer-term value-prepping benefits and will pursue this easy and beneficial process.

By the very nature of being in business, an owners' path to strategic success is rife with risk. Life can go sideways in seconds, beyond a client's control, which can result in impaired value and potential loss of the entire business. It happened to me as an owner at a critical transition point in my career, as you will learn in the next chapter. One of the built-in benefits of value-prepping is being value-protected against such chance events.

The risk of missing one little detail during the execution of a strategic big move can torpedo your clients' vision. We know from experience *ad hoc* management of the process leads to missed steps. That is why your clients need you as their guide as well as a system to manage it all—from strategic opportunity to valuation to transaction, transition or transformation. It is all designed to ensure your clients reach their vision.

The goal for any business owner is clear: PROTECT YOUR VISION with the RIGHT PREPARATION and take the RIGHT STEPS. In today's world of high speed, elevated risk and layers of complexity, value-prepping is a relevant topic at the forefront of discussion with any business owner. When a business is unprepared, the consequences of not value-prepping can be devastating emotionally and financially. Unfortunately, it is not only your client, but their loved ones who may also suffer the consequences of unfavorable events.

Before you introduce value-prepping and true value to your clients as a new way of thinking about business value, this book will provide you with four valuable lessons. First, it will dispel any mystery surrounding finding, building and protecting true value in a business. Second, it will show you what a constant state of business readiness associated with the value-prepping process brings to a client. Third, it will provide you with the tools you need to make your clients feel confident in their strategic decisions and peace of mind that their business can withstand chance events. Finally, it will reveal the potential for adding real value to your clients' future business wealth.

Together we can positively impact your client's business and their family in a way you have never imagined possible.

Are you ready?

David Wayne Wimer

CHAPTER ONE

A CAREER WITH VALUE

LESSONS OF BUSINESS OWNERSHIP

After a 40+ year career, I was ready to leave the corporate world. I was impatient and felt compelled to strike out on the entrepreneur's path with a co-founder with whom I would remain partners for 20 years. From that point on, I became self-employed for the rest of my career. Beginning in 1977, we started up, owned and operated businesses in six different industries: direct B2B sales, staffing services, software application development, and network technology, metals manufacturing, franchise, and last-mile logistics. My business ownership journey did not occur in a straight line, smooth or clear. It was a zig-zag from one sector to another. I craved new challenges and new experiences. I was willing to learn because I was always curious about the next challenge. An education always costs time or money. In my instance, I invested in both.

Throughout my ownership experiences since age 23, I navigated and survived five major economic recession periods. It was during these times I recognized it was much easier to start a business than to stay in business.

- 1980-1982 (raising of interest rates to combat inflation, high unemployment, and Iranian oil embargo)
- 1990-1991 (savings and loan crisis)
- 2001 (dot.com bust, unemployment and 9/11)
- 2007-2009 (the Great Recession and bank credit crisis)
- 2020-2022 (eye of the pandemic and trailing recession)

In my early years, overcoming market challenges and economic changes to earn a living was satisfying, although it took a lot of energy. I learned as I built various companies and took them through the start-up-to-sale life cycles. I had not learned two key business wealth-building lessons—how to build value in the business and how to make it transferable. *What I did not realize at the time resulted in leaving one or two handsome retirements on the table when exiting a couple of businesses.*

Although I was extremely resourceful as an entrepreneur, that quality led me at times to wade into deep waters, and oftentimes, swift currents. Some things I did well in business when navigating the rapids, and others I did not so well, which thankfully I recognized most times before it was too late and I went underwater. That was until a chance event occurred: Y2K.

In 1998, a computer flaw, the so-called "Millennium Bug," led to widespread tech anxiety and the Y2K (Year 2000) scare. As the year 2000 approached, many corporations believed that existing computer systems would not interpret the "00" correctly, causing a major glitch in the largest of legacy data and Enterprise Resource Planning (ERP) systems. By mid-July 1998, major projects in the sales pipeline of my six-year-old software development company focused on multi-million-dollar electronic document management systems integrated with these ERP systems also stalled.

With multi-million-dollar projects delayed indefinitely, and a high monthly operating burn rate, my owner world came to a screeching halt. Had I been prepared with working capital I would have been able to overcome the resultant 18-month delay and had the potential to flourish with a $24 million dollar opportunity in the wings. Instead, I did not have the capital, nor was the company diversified enough to withstand a forward-looking 24-month float to pay for operations. It was a classic case of being unprepared for sudden chance events. I had built up the necessary talent pool to execute on large enterprise-wide contracts in anticipation of contract engagements. Without the talent, there would be no business opportunities in the future. By the end of 1998, I was forced to sell the business.

At the same time, I was asked by a local CEO of a 50-year-old, second generation contract packaging business to recover a $750,000 manufacturing ERP system gone haywire. Inventories were not accurate and therefore failing lender asset validation and Line of Credit access limit verification. On one hand, I was engaging in what I thought would be a major leap in my technical re-engineering and workflow process consulting prowess. On the other hand, I was in the midst of liquidating my prized business to the software toolkit company we represented. It was a time of bittersweet irony.

Within 60 days I led the manufacturer's management team through a systems analysis, froze the software developer's code changes, identified the gaps in process, and had inventories accurately stated for the lenders and borrowing base calculations. At the same time, my systems integration company was sold with the unbelievable talent I had attracted. I was heartbroken in the transition. But I was grateful for the immediate opportunity to help another owner with something I knew intimately. With no crystal ball on my career, or next steps, my first turnaround opportunity materialized.

LEARNING FROM TURNAROUNDS

What I did not see as an owner/operator in my first 20 years in business I began to discover as a turnaround executive over the next 6 years. Starting with the ERP recovery and immersing myself in manufacturing and distribution, I found many of my lessons learned as an entrepreneur were applicable as a hired interim turnaround executive leading another owner's business finance and operations teams.

As a turnaround executive, I led businesses in deep financial trouble caused by poor owner choices, neglect of fundamentals of financial accountability and inconsistent management. The businesses were mired in poor leadership, fragmented direction, flavor-of-the-day decisions coupled with negative, chance events that occurred beyond anyone's control. You might call it the perfect storm for a business catastrophe!

These opportunities deepened my understanding of troubled company financing and exit options. With revenue from $12 million to $100 million in revenue, I was leading companies that had lost their way. One company was losing 10% of revenue and another was hemorrhaging upwards to $7.0 million a year. Somehow, in the worst of circumstances during my executive leadership, things turned out for the best for those companies and owners.

Achieving a turn towards profitability is no easy task, especially when the company has deep-rooted inertia. The challenges seemed simple enough: lower the water (costs) or raise the bridge (revenues). In one case, both needed to be accomplished at the same time. Turnarounds gave me an opportunity to see how other business owners behaved under pressure, and how each owner responded differently to crises in their business. That offered insights into how each business had become troubled.

Some owners were at their best and others were at their worst in these pressure-charged situations. All had budgets and forecasts, but not one business owner had systematically prepared any strategic plan to address options and contingencies during periods of change. All were concentrating on operations and drivers of revenue and profitability. All had lost sight of impacts on cash flow and value. All faced significant changes in their business and their personal lives in the process of returning the business to normalcy. One, unbeknownst to me, was a few weeks from bankruptcy when I arrived on the scene. At the time, it was good I did not know it, or I may not have accepted the assignment. In any case, with the forced sale of my prized business, I knew exactly how a significant loss felt as an owner, which motivated me to help.

My leadership approach was simple: people first, always. Lead with heart, then minds and hands would follow. My financial approach was equally simple: focus on cash flow and value. The outcome of each assignment was a successful sale. One company even sold to a NYSE traded, publicly held strategic customer. Throughout, I documented my experiences and obtained further education in turnaround knowledge and finance. Each new skill was applied to the next opportunity. Which led me to ask myself, *why had these companies failed, when all had once been profitable with significant revenues?*

Oftentimes, I wondered how these businesses and their owners had been lucky enough to overcome insurmountable odds of survival. Had they continued the same behaviors before I arrived, the businesses certainly would have been liquidated. In each case, once the assignment concluded, I noted what steps I had taken and the key changes that occurred internally and externally. Most importantly, I recognized how each of those businesses was turned around financially to eventually become valuable assets to sell for the family business owners. They were remarkable successes. I knew I was on to something more than met the eye. The business preparation picture was blurry, but my instincts told me to give it time.

INSIGHTS FROM A FAMILY OFFICE

What happened to me next was fortuitous. I was introduced by a long-time friend to a high-net-worth family member at a time when I least expected it—on vacation. This was the beginning of my family office work. The financial stakes were higher than I ever could have imagined for these clients. They faced multiple devastating events over five years. The first was a chance economic event, the Great Recession of 2007-2009. That one event placed their entire portfolio of operating assets in jeopardy of liquidation.

The second concurrent chance event that occurred was the mental health disability of a co-founder, which set off a chain of other partnership rifts that impacted the business' profitability. Disagreement reigned between general partners, family members became estranged, critical franchise licenses were terminated, the divorce of a co-founder, and death of another co-founder became more fuel for the financial fire.

Through sheer perseverance, relying on my intuitive business instincts and practical experiences, I applied what I had learned as a business owner and in-house turnaround executive. Collaborating with the co-owner's long-time CPA's and legal counsel, we navigated through treacherous chance events. That included franchise license termination, dangerously low cash flow and short loan maturity terms that constrained cash flow. Avoiding crises with strategic planning and financing skills, I was able to guide the family's business assets to double their value in five years. The owners were delighted. They decided it was time to de-risk and execute an exit, which I was prepared to lead. It was a remarkable success, and a chapter of my career I would never forget. I learned more than I had anticipated when I agreed to review that one purchase agreement, and saved the family from a $2.2 million wrong decision, as the offer price had been undervalued.

Diving deeper into how this transformation had occurred gave me pause. As I replayed the big picture options we created and the spouses' right decisions, I realized there were elements of a preparation process beginning to take shape. My next step in M&A would be helpful in connecting the missing pieces of the business readiness and value puzzle.

VALUE IN M&A WORK

If my family office experiences taught me about cash flow and company value, my M&A work helped me see readiness themes and elements of preparation morph into a process. Our M&A firm served the privately held business sector with values from $2 million to $50 million. Contingency means we were paid only if we were successful. That was a huge risk as any given transaction took 800-1200 hours of work over 9 to 18 months by our team. We needed to be sure that we could deliver on the engagement in order to be paid. Now that takes grit and confidence!

As an M&A Advisor I gained a firsthand perspective on the importance of value when a company was supposedly "ready" for market. None were actually prepared. None had anticipated the difficulties that arose during every sale process. Our role was to educate the owner and to guide them through the oftentimes grueling and frustrating aspects of the M&A sale process. Once the price and general terms had been agreed upon, the real work began. Internal or external pressures the owners were feeling complicated the process further. The former managing partner of our firm, Bob McCormack said it best, "Ten percent of this selling process is financial. Ninety percent of the process is navigating the most emotional rollercoaster the client has ever ridden."

As an underwriter, I was responsible for analysis, valuation, testing market values, writing the offering memorandum, packaging the company for market, and doing pre-market due diligence. In the next phase of a transaction, post letter-of-intent, I would collaborate with the owner, the management team, transaction attorney, and accounting and tax professionals from both buyer and seller. This opportunity gave me a broad and deep perspective on what both parties were desiring to achieve, the buildup of value, value gap analysis, owner outcome desires, and business readiness for prime-time sale. A key to maximizing price was transferability of business value to the buyer for expected growth.

I analyzed the values of hundreds of companies as an underwriter and talked directly with owners about their operations and financials. As I searched for clues to provide objective market value insight, Ben Franklin's timeless wisdom *"an ounce of prevention is worth a pound of cure"* echoed true. Nine out of ten businesses were not ready for prime-time sale.

What I found over time was half of those unprepared businesses would never sell or transfer. These were lifestyle businesses whose owners either started them to fulfill a spending need, bought a business due to an early retirement, or wanted the freedom to make an above average living, rather than remain an employee. Not surprisingly, lifestyle businesses were not value-building enterprises. These owners would drain business cash flow to meet personal spending needs. Therefore, with no value built, the businesses were not transferable. These selling opportunities were often classified as "turn downs" for representation. The likelihood was we would invest hundreds of hours on contingency with no reward for doing so, frustrating the owner and our team.

For the remaining half of those unprepared business cases, we openly discussed their business' "readiness" to go to market and offered the option to delay the process until they were prepared. Imagine the decision those owners faced. They were already stressed considering a sale and transition in their personal lives. Many had fantasized about a big payday and had started to investigate how they would spend it. Of the remaining half, only one company would commit to delaying a sale and preparing for this critical step before going to market. We would assist by monitoring their value over a one-to-two-year period, providing guidance along the way.

Our approach to guidance emanated from the collective wisdom among our team of seasoned advisors that included former business owners, corporate CEO's and bankers. We were positively impacting the outcome each time, but there was no repeatable process available to follow. To me this approach did not seem to be enough, given that outcomes were affecting the lives of owners and their families who were doing this only once in a lifetime.

ADDRESSING & BRIDGING VALUE GAPS

A Value Gap existed in most unprepared business cases between expectations of the owner and pricing realities in their industry or market. Ten percent of owners embraced our offer to prepare and received practical advice that shaped positive returns. Value-prepping relationships lasted 1 to 2 years, depending upon the scope of preparation required. Each company had unique needs and areas of their business to value-prep. We provided insights and held quarterly conference calls to review internal progress in their journey of preparation. I noticed the owners who adopted the process became educated in and diligently committed to increasing value in their businesses. They realized the benefits. The outcomes of preparation were starting to pay off in higher pricing multiples.

At the same time, I considered how I could transform what we intrinsically knew from our collective experiences and turn it into a predictable process. Anecdotally, my experience and education told me there could be upwards of 1.20X lift to a business' selling price if an M&A team of professionals led the sale process. I posited that the remaining ninety percent of businesses, whose value was negative to neutral, could re-orient and build value. With redirection and using key questions, the business owner could do it.

We did not have all the answers. Rather, it was our disciplined approach in questioning which allowed us to provide guidance to the owners which increased measurable value by increasing EBITDA, which in turn increased the Fair Market Value of their company with higher multiples.For an owner who typically has up to 85% of their personal wealth invested and locked inside the business, maximizing life-long business value has rare significance. It also struck me that owners wanted and needed to be educated on their true value and how to go about finding, building and protecting wealth in their businesses. Like any change we make in our personal lives, I also recognized value-prepping would be easier with a coach as a guide.

SIMPLIFIED VALUE-PREP® IS BORN

My hypothesis on using business preparation and readiness to improve value was tested in several live cases as an M&A

advisor. I globally observed: *the more prepared a business, the more likely it would be sold for a higher value.*

It is said that to be a good teacher, you need to be a good student. In 2019, after accepting an offer to create and teach my first live course for M&A Source, a national M&A Association, I researched topics extensively. What I agreed to deliver was *How to Prepare a Business for Sale to Maximize Value.* I designed the course with Simplified Value-Prep® as its core process for the purpose of the sale of a business to a third party. What had been percolating for years regarding value culminated in this proprietary design. The accumulation of my experiences as a business owner, turnaround executive, Family Office and M&A Advisor provided fertile ground to germinate this four-step value-prepping process known as the COACH Method™ for business readiness.

After formally introducing Simplified Value-Prep® in 2019 to fellow M&A Advisors, I taught the course again in 2020. Simplified Value-Prep® is a path any business owner can easily follow. Recall our earlier metaphor in finding buried treasure? Simplified Value-Prep® is the owner's "map" to true value. The COACH Method™ (Calculate, Orient, Adapt, CHoose) are the four steps to follow and complete. They are the actions to "dig" for true value in the right spot. In fact, the initial tasks of collecting the necessary documents for Calculating true value are easily handled by any trusted CFO, Controller or Executive Assistant. The owner is reserved for strategic analysis and decision-making.

With a Value Advisor as a guide, Simplified Value-Prep® keeps the business owner on the right path with the right information to execute their vision for the life of the business. A constant state of business readiness protects that treasure they have worked so hard to find and build.

THE THEORY OF READINESS™ MATERIALIZES

The eureka moment to formalize my *Theory of Readiness*™ occurred after teaching Simplified Value-Prep® in 2020. With an offer to teach it again in May 2022, *Theory of Readiness's* universal purpose came to me in the form of a novella which I wrote for business owners. *The Tale of Mac & Murphy* tells the story of Murphy, an unprepared business owner struggling with an unforeseen, looming business crisis. In contrast to Murphy's dilemma, his cousin Mac's business value is value-protected by his wisdom of preparedness, offering him options when they count most.

My *Theory of Readiness*™ applies to preparing *any business to be in a constant state of readiness for whatever events may occur, by choice or by chance.* Actionable goals build value and insulate the business, protecting long-term business wealth. *Theory of Readiness*™ is supported anecdotally and quantitatively. By measuring change in value over a brief period of time, an owner sees value build with the leverage of a multiple. By mitigating risks to reach a readiness state, a prepared value is further protected. That part of the process makes timing irrelevant and de-risks the negative impact of chance events. The underlying process for creating business readiness, Simplified Value-Prep®, supports the *Theory of Readiness*™ by identifying and quantifying the True Value of the business. The processes lead to answering the right questions required to de-risk the business and create valuable contingencies and options.

Every owner who has avoided a business crisis or catastrophe can appreciate the priceless effect of readiness protection when confronted with a chance negative event. Not only are crises emotionally draining for the entire company, but they are equally damaging when options are limited. Having peace of mind that the business is in a ready state provides decision support and confidence. It is easier to make the right decision when faced with any creative or critical situation—an acquisition, a new investment in product lines, analysis of a competitor's offer to buy you, or when unforeseen chance events portend a crisis. That is why the most crucial decision the business owner faces in our world of growing complexity is: to Value-Prep, or not to Value-Prep? By using Simplified Value-Prep® as a tool, your business owner clients find and build true value and protect their business wealth.

THE ERA OF VALUE ADVISING

I see a new era where complexities drive rapid decisions to maintain a competitive edge. Many owners have lost invested capital and confidence in the past two years of the Coronavirus Pandemic. But there is no time to surrender. It is time to take advantage of new ways of being prepared for both challenges and opportunities. That is why I am building out a network of educated Value Advisors intent on finding, building and protecting true value. My intent is to help business owners create new business wealth. These same owners have worked so hard to survive, it is their time to once again flourish. Before outlining the case for business readiness in the next chapter, I want to share my background, experience and certifications that make me uniquely qualified to lead in this value-oriented era.

I am not licensed in securities, accounting or law nor would I attempt to practice these professions without the education, experience and certifications required. That is your role. My Value Advisory work has always been aligned with the goals of business owners in concert with their professional advisors—wealth managers, certified financial planners, insurance representatives, investment bankers, commercial real estate brokers, M&A advisors, attorneys, and accountants. My role as deal underwriter, collaborator and facilitator required a broad knowledge of each professionals' role as they related to the business owner and their wealth-producing assets. Understanding the intricacies of what each professional brings to an owner is how I was able to orchestrate incredibly challenging and rewarding turnaround and transactional successes. It is also important to understand how I reached this point in my advisory career.

My more formal education as an M&A advisor includes many hours of continuing education in nationally accredited courses. The certifications I have earned, my success in advising clients on true value, and my educational path in teaching peers has earned me Fellow status with the largest association of M&A professionals in the globe, the M&A Source (masource.org). This is the professional education I rely upon to advise other advisors in their use of Simplified Value-Prep®.

My goal in *The Advisor's Guide to Business Wealth* is to provide these unique insights to you and your business owner clients. This is a new way for you to solicit, attract and convert new business owner clients for your practice. By prescribing this practical tool, Simplified Value-Prep®, your clients will succeed in finding, building and protecting the true value of their businesses. The opportunity in this post-pandemic era of Value Advising is ripe. The most important decision your business owner clients will ever make is: to Value-Prep, or not to Value-Prep? It is my hope you can be leading that conversation.

CHAPTER TWO

THE CASE FOR BUSINESS READINESS

Often I have heard the following from clients, *"I'm just amazed. If I had to find someone like you, I don't know where I would go out and look."* Or others have told me, *"I didn't know a service even existed like this one. We are so lucky we found you when we did."*

For most business owners, Google just doesn't cut it as a way to reach an advisor with the requisite insight and experiences the client needs. That is, if the client actually knows what is in their business' best interests. Sometimes bias and blind spots hold back a client from adopting any new process or divergent thinking. The mindset of a business owner will be addressed in the next chapter. Like the concept of business readiness, the unknown can be fearful to us, difficult to admit what we do not know. However, on the other side of that coin is a most powerful vulnerability that leads to finding new methods and attaining new levels of success. When we acknowledge the unknown and embrace our resistance, surrender opens up our minds to abundance. That may be the perfect backdrop for the case for business readiness.

Many who advise others do so quietly, behind the scenes, and without fanfare. Due to the confidentiality involved, we know we cannot promote our work specifically regarding any one client. We never disclose names due to privacy rules and professional discretion. Our reputations and integrity need to remain impeccable. Many times, with the approval of our client, we are referred by a trusted, competent, and interest-vested colleague, who may see a need developing and a fit for our services. As it is with introducing anything new, the first steps are building that bridge of understanding to earn trust in adoption. Simplified Value-Prep® is no different with the opportunities it holds for your current and future clients.

HOW MUCH CAN A CLIENT EXPECT IN RETURN?

Likely, this question has been surfacing as you have been reading. A specific answer depends upon unique factors about your clients' business which are uncovered during the process and the primary reason to use Simplified Value-Prep®. The minimum goal of business preparation is to increase EBITDA (Earnings Before Interest Taxes & Depreciation) by a minimum of 1X. The calculation is simple. If your business has a Fair Market Value of four times (known as the Multiple) times EBITDA, and you raise that four times by 1X to 5X EBITDA because you are prepared and have things in order making the business more attractive to the marketplace, you have increased your return by 25%. For example, if your EBITDA is $500,000 @ 4X = $2,000,000 and value-prepping yields you an additional $500,000, wouldn't you be pleased? The impacts of increasing multiples are substantial.

In addition to Simplified Value-Prep® being designed to build value, there is an intrinsic benefit of preparation that protects value. The resultant readiness state is like having built-in "self-insurance" to protect value when faced with sudden events. The self-insuring aspect acts as a tool for strategic decision support. You might think of it as icing on the cake.

For example, there may be an acquisition that suddenly appears, which would catapult your growth. Unless you have done your value-prepping homework on your own business, how can you responsibly respond and rapidly purchase another one? Should a sudden crisis occur, knowing what options and contingencies you have as they relate to the value of your business is critical. Thinking through contingencies beforehand can keep you steps ahead of any potential crisis. As a turnaround colleague once asked, "Why would anyone pay double, triple or five times more to get out of trouble, when with a small investment of time in thoughtful planning, trouble can be mitigated or avoided altogether?" That same outlook applies to value-prepping a client's business.

In business we pay for general, property, casualty, EPLI, medical, life, and disability insurance premiums throughout the life of the business, for situations which may never occur. We accept without question the insurance model as a necessity for being in business to protect against any number of calamities. Yet, many business owners resist the modest investment of time involved in value-prepping their businesses, where they can obtain real increases in business wealth. I agree it is much easier to ignore value-prepping and do nothing. However, that one decision inevitably takes its toll on eventual selling price and limits options during a crisis. So why place that hard-earned value at risk in the first place?

With time as the real enemy to achievement, having options is priceless. Simplified Value-Prep® allows clients the peace of mind to know they have considered the value impact of their strategic decisions, regardless of whether it is a sudden crisis event or a golden egg opportunity. Their Value-Prep Plan becomes the instrumental decision support tool as their business faces complexity, change, and its future.

POOR TIMING YIELDS POOR RESULTS

From a business owner's view, there is never a convenient time to learn and integrate something new into the business. Even more significant than inconvenience is that the odds of success are not stacked in your client's favor. At the exact moment when a client may need high value the most, it may be elusive. After investing countless hours, years, capital, and personal energy into their business, they may be left with nothing to show for it but debt and liabilities. They may have lost an income stream and the lifestyle they enjoyed. I assure you, if they choose to Value-Prep and use it as a measurement of financial success, being in a constant state of readiness will protect this asset they have worked so hard to build. Your clients can act on any one of the four strategies, RENEW, BUILD, BUY, or SELL with confidence. They will be prepared to face both challenges and opportunity. Once readied, the business will carry them to achievements of which they have always dreamed. It only takes a little time to gain a lot of clarity.

A savvy and responsible owner usually wants as much information ahead of a strategic business move. They may have been considering it for some time without revealing it to others. An owner wants to understand the risks involved *before* making a commitment of capital and resources. Therefore, a key question to ask is, *what is the context for the strategic decision being made by the owner? Is it in the context of knowing one's own value, before taking on the challenge of executing any of the four aforementioned strategic actions?* That is where Simplified Value-Prep® can be utilized most effectively.

For instance, owners frequently assume the strategic decision to BUY is accretive, and many times that assumption can be flawed. According to an article in Harvard Business Review titled *Don't Make This M&A Mistake* by Graham Kenney (June 2020), between 70% and 90% of post-sale integrations fail to provide their initial intended benefits. What is even more interesting is that Mr. Kenney notes the severity of post-sale integration failure is higher when the acquisition is of a complementary organization.

As you can see it is critical not to miss the blind spot of looking inside and outside the owners' business, before executing any strategic actions. That includes the often-overlooked intangibles and hidden value. The odds of success in these strategic instances are actually not in the owner's favor unless they are prepared. Simplified Value-Prep® de-risks these strategic actions using its proprietary process. By simplifying complex steps and unveiling hidden ones, the owner's vision of accumulating business wealth becomes actionable and improves their odds of a successful outcome.

OPENING THE DOOR TO POSSIBILITIES

Many times, the demands of operating a business do not allow an owner the time to step back and see the business from other vantage points, or to develop expertise in specialized business areas. In fact, most owners have never considered how a state of readiness can be a strategic tool. That is where you as a Value Advisor can fill in the knowledge and experience gap by tapping your core education and experiences with a diverse group of businesses, and apply it to the owner's business case. Advisors in general can help owners to ideate and find new possibilities that may never have occurred should the owner remain alone and focused on the daily management of their business. In other words, it is the advisor's role to remain "outside the box," unconstrained by the "conventional wisdom" in any specific industry. That is also how Simplified Value-Prep® can be universally applied.

With the goal of business readiness in mind, it is important that owners do not surrender to the temptation to cut corners or ignore strategic planning altogether. Value-prepping takes a financial perspective. While retaining consultants in the same industry may be wise for executing specific tasks such as engineering, lean thinking, or other industry-specific reasons, an owner must look outside their industry for a Value Advisor. Objective perspective requires differences. At the same time, the Value Advisor needs to establish trust based on a number of factors such as education, certifications, experience, delivery of outcomes, and uncompromised integrity. Owners also need to strike a balance between what they may want, and what is right for the business.

CHAPTER THREE

THE MINDSET OF AN OWNER

As advisors we invest much time in learning subject-matter expertise, self-development, and professional education to ensure we are performing at our best for any business owner. When selecting an advisor, owners depend upon credentialing and compliance to written and unwritten standards. As advisors we have one virtue that must always remain unblemished—our reputation. Our professional referrals also depend upon it. Integrity is paramount to acquiring and maintaining an uncompromised client relationship.

An advisor's role is one of providing decision support in the form of research, analysis and considerations for the owner to weigh. It is always up to the owner to make the final decision and to execute their selected decision. Once advice is provided, the advisor is strictly hands-off on execution, there to observe and provide feedback to the owner. An advisor can respectfully "speak truth to power" when appropriate. In the end, the owner must live with and remain accountable for the consequences of any decision.

Referrals are the lifeblood of our profession. They come from other professionals we have collaborated with, and from satisfied clients. You have heard or seen this adage, *"The greatest compliment you can give is your trusted referral of another."* To earn trust, we must always deliver the utmost care for our client's vision and goals.

BUILDING OWNER TRUST

An advisor in financial matters has a fiduciary duty to clients. Fiduciary duty includes a duty of loyalty and a duty of care. A fiduciary duty is a commitment to act in the best interests of another person or entity. That means, the advisor must act diligently with the highest level of scrutiny and care not to harm. It is likely this is something we share in common with clients. Partners also have this duty of care to one another. It is the highest level of trust that one may find in any business structure. The business owner gets a better result from an advisor who is committed to what is in their best interests and what's right for the business, not necessarily what is easy or what the owner may want to hear, see, or do.

At times, this fiduciary duty may come at a cost to our earnings. As an example, in one M&A case we had a cash deal of $4 million and the owners became concerned about their decision to sell. It was a complex case to start with: interwoven for-profit and non-profit companies. This particular situation taught me a valuable lesson in preparation. In the 11th hour, the sellers, husband-and-wife co-owners, decided not to sell. That decision came after our firm invested 18 months and hundreds of hours of time and talent. They did not feel the corporate strategic buyer would be a good fit long-term. What was my response when their CPA asked what they owed us? *Nothing.* Our integrity overrode any income or default provision. We were engaged on contingency. That moment never materialized. We moved on to serving our other active clients.

Skeptics by profession, a business owner must develop respect and confidence that an advisor can help them get what they want, before trust is earned. Education is one method to doing so. Most owners do not wish to be sold. Owners want to hear the bottom line to save their time. Anything meaningful that could rock their world positively or negatively is something of value. Instinctively an owner can sense an imposter. They use an internal meter that is very refined. Therefore, an advisor must be authentic.

There is no room in the advisory business for *"Yes, always,"* or the faint of heart. Before overzealously entering choppy waters, I would offer a word of caution. Whether or not an owner is willing to attempt something out of their comfort zone depends upon the trust that has been built with the advisor. The advisor must ease the owners' fears by providing justifications, or the needed changes will not be made. That trust must be built before there is even an attempt to embark on a risky, but needed, course of action. Otherwise, the owner's concentration will be on what they might lose, not on what they might gain. The larger the needed transformation, the more likely it will be that results may get worse before they get better. Sustainable change always takes time. An experienced advisor will build owner confidence by focusing on little successes along the way.

Finally, there is a need for the advisor to be aware of his or her own limitations. For instance, the advisor's lesser industry knowledge may be a valid blind spot, depending upon their purpose. Credit the owner with knowing what they are doing in their area of subject-matter expertise. The advisor needs to be truthful when providing options to the owner that are unproven or risky. There is the *caveat* that the advisor may not have a valid perspective due to a limitation of industry-specific knowledge. In fact, the owner may have a more pertinent or relevant understanding which may not make complete sense to the advisor. Communicating openly about the above give-and-take of knowledge and experience usually establishes additional trust between the owner and an advisor.

INFORMAL NETWORKS

The first place a typical owner goes to for advice is their informal network. Informal networks may include:

1. Spouse or Significant Other
2. Another Family Member
3. Key Employee or Partner
4. Business Colleague
5. The "Buddy" System

Informal networks are usually convenient, comfortable and readily accessible. They are so integrated into work life that they do not really get noticed. They just happen naturally. These informal networks provide the owner with an opportunity to discuss common problems on the surface, and to bounce ideas and concepts off friends they trust. However, informal networks provide no accountability. A person in the owner's informal network knows the owner in a certain setting, so they may not feel comfortable giving the owner honest, hard-to-hear advice.

Informal networks have built-in subjectivity. The question for the owner is this: *can you actually get to the hard truth, or do you have to put on an appearance? Conversely, does the informal network feel a need to protect you or shield you from the hard truth? Do they become so subjective that they cannot see the hard truth, themselves?* Each of the above informal sources for advice also have a tradeoff. Confidentiality cannot always be assured. When relationships are intertwined with making the right business decision, total honesty may be hard to come by, depending upon the topic.

Quite typically, the owner utilizes informal sources for casual talk and testing some of their thoughts on daily matters that may be percolating. The close friend "Buddy" model may include a regular time where the owner can relax and talk while enjoying an activity like golf, tennis, fishing, or hunting partners in an unrelated field. Sometimes, owners have built enough trust with a friend or associate to discuss their concerns in greater detail. This allows the owner to "vent" their fears and concerns in an environment they consider safe. By talking things through in greater depth and detail with a trusted friend in a confidential setting, potential solutions might emerge.

However, talking it through aloud without an honest listener may produce the effect of an owner answering their own questions and listening to their own answers. Again, subjectivity is involved. And their frame of reference has not changed at all. The problem may require a differing perspective. That's where an advisor's role becomes invaluable.

FORMAL NETWORKS

Formal networks may consist of a local or regional group the owner has joined for the purpose of sharing experiences and best practices, or as a way for self-development to occur in a safe environment. These are normally confidential forums designed for business owners to belong, share ideas, and experiences and to enjoy the benefits of networking with other owners. There are organizations that provide more formalized networking support. These include Vistage, YPO, YEO, WEO, TAB, and the Chief Executive Network. Self-developmental progress can be made in these settings where a "forum" of owners use their skills to help another owner through questioning. What the owner wants is a safe environment where confidentiality exists and where they can source wisdom from business colleagues in whom they can trust.

When the triggering problem is more threatening or there is a defined objective such as renewing a business, building for growth, charting succession, consideration of a sale or contemplating an acquisition, an owner will seek more formal guidance. At these times, informal or even formal networks may not be acceptable. It may be a highly confidential and strategic big move, or a situation related to the owner's business outlook such as a looming crisis, financial performance, or even their deepest inner conflicts or fears about failure and continuance. In these cases, the owner needs more professional input. Typically, that is where a professional advisor can help.

WHY OWNERS MAY RESIST ADVICE

It would be wonderful if advisors would provide their analysis and owners would simply do as advised. I have never seen it happen. In advisory situations, owners are uncomfortable, even afraid. They want to be sure they are doing the right thing. With experiences comes a level of healthy skepticism. There are always a number of the ways that an advisory process can go wrong. The purpose here is to alert advisors to these potential dangers so that they can be avoided.

There are a host of reasons why an owner may resist. Let us start out first with the dilemma and paradox of ownership. By their mere position as owner or founder, followers naturally *expect* their owner to have all the answers. It is their baby, money and time. That reasoning could not be farther from the truth. The dilemmas faced by owners start with their belief system, in particular, their "limiting beliefs." Limiting beliefs are the judgments we make about ourselves and our situations that limit our capability to act.

Another reason some owners avoid retaining an advisor is the axiom, *"Once bitten, twice shy."* They, or someone they trust, may have had an unpleasant experience in the past, and the bitterness of the fleecing lasts forever. Unfortunately, there are a lot of imposters out there pretending to be advisors, with unproven systems, who do not know what they are doing. Imposters make it more difficult to build owner trust for those of us who are verifiably motivated, competent and qualified to help. I have had the humiliating experience of engaging an imposter consultant with a personal agenda. At the time, my pain was far greater than the development of my radar. It was a difficult $20,000 pill to swallow. I learned from that one experience to outline what I wanted as the basis for any engagement. Over time I learned how to vet future consultants and advisors. The point I am making is this – do not let one unpleasant experience keep you from obtaining the benefit of so many valuable advisors. Likewise, do not allow one owner's resistance to deter you from bringing light to something you believe is helpful.

THE TRICKS OF EGO

Our ego has a way of tricking us any time we go to solve a complex problem. There is a little voice in our head that makes a statement and then asks a question. *I have done it before, why shouldn't I be able to do it again? Why would someone else be able to do it better?* I have seen this do-it-yourself, John

Wayne attitude in many successful owners. With honesty, I can look at the man-in-the-mirror and confess. My early days as an owner were driven by similar thoughts. Some owners believe denying the realities they face may make them go away. Others may believe they got themselves into trouble and only they can get themselves out. That flaw only contributes to extensive suffering when it could be solved by objective insight.

As we have seen from our advisor's vantage point, a self-reliant attitude may only work when the situation is exactly the same as it was at some time in the past. We already know nothing in the business world ever stays the same. In fact, some of the biggest changes never seen before in our business world are occurring right now in the current economic climate. That tells us as owners we need to be adaptable and armed with the latest tools. We also must recognize as business owners that the owners' ego is a tricky protection device. Ego has difficulty accepting the possibility that someone else might be as capable or have the right potential answers outside of it. Keeping ego in check helps owners deal with the realities they face can be a major hurdle to making progress if unchecked In this process of interdependence, collaboration and working together.

As advisors, we presume that the owner knows what they are doing technically. Otherwise, they would not even *be* in business. The advisor's role is to help with decision support as a guide so that the owner can overcome their present difficulties and *stay* in business. Many owners go into business for themselves because they believe they know better than anyone else. And that works well, especially when knowing better means improvement in delivery of goods or services to gain a competitive edge.

Given areas of technical or industry-specific knowledge, most owners do know better than others. It is quite possible that the owner's technical knowledge was what initially allowed them their start in business. But ego may prevent them from understanding what they do not know, which may fall outside their area of immediate subject-matter expertise. What they do not know can end up being very costly to them personally. One small business detail, like forgetting to confront nexus in inter-state commerce, or adopting a flawed job-costing accounting for work in progress and labor can be value killers. And that is our role to help uncover as an advisor.

FIRE, AIM, FIRE

Business owners tend to be people compelled more towards action than strategy. In general, they would rather DO, than think about doing. Engaging an advisor to help think through a situation before acting can seem like a waste of time and money to an owner facing a crisis they're in a hurry to resolve. Oftentimes, their approach is like the title of this chapter: all in the wrong order.

Advisors are valuable for filling in the gaps and blind spots an owner may miss. With Simplified Value-Prep® for instance our approach is AIM, READY, FIRE. To an owner, that may mean we are torturing them with detail upfront. For us, it is detail that gets desired strategic outcomes. Knowing the owner's propensity for action *before* introducing a new system or process is helpful. That means you understand how the owner may be perceiving the work ahead. You can address and set the expectations early on what needs to be done to gain the desired state. None of it is difficult. It is just new to the owner. In that light, an owner may resist a little or a lot at the beginning. So, what they really want is to understand and justify moving ahead.

I CANNOT AFFORD IT

The final overwhelming source of resistance is that business advice is a luxury and the business cannot afford it. That thinking is especially prevalent when things are not going well. This is the old roof repair paradox. When it is not raining, a leaky roof is not a problem, so it is not top of mind, gets ignored, and does not get fixed. Then when it is raining, it becomes too risky to climb up onto the wet roof to fix it, so the roof does not get fixed. Therefore, the roof never gets fixed. The long-term problem is that below the roof, the house starts to deteriorate from the water and eventually the cost to operate becomes vastly higher than the fix would have been in the first place.

It is also impossible to measure what a return on investment an advisor will bring when the problem and solution have not been fully defined. Business owners understand that cash flow is king. We preserve assets and preserve cash flow for clients every day. When talking to troubled business

THE ADVISOR'S GUIDE TO BUSINESS WEALTH

owners, I ask, *can you afford NOT to get some professional advice here? What are the negative consequences of continuing to do the same thing and getting the same results? What are the risks of making a big mistake at this critical time?* Once we have quantified potential risks and rewards, it is much easier to provide the owner a compelling proposal.

Advisory services are calculated investments for an expected return. In one engagement, I helped the owner sell a profitable portion of a business and close the remaining portion so the owner could retire. In that engagement, I returned more than seven times the investment the owner made in me, much more value than he had previously anticipated. When we started, the owner thought he had a qualified buyer in the corral which was a large institution. At face value, that buyer may have appeared to be the best exit solution due to its size and resources. His ideal buyer had never closed a strategic acquisition. You guessed it! I already knew that was a dead end based on the buyer's inexperience. Instead, we needed to prove the owner's misconception while I found the right buyer who saw the true value in the strategic acquisition. By virtue of getting the deal done, that owner is a friend for life.

Owners are better suited to see justification for engaging advisors when that engagement is viewed as an investment rather than an expense. I can easily relate to showing a client a return of an additional 1X EBITDA from our work together. That one time may represent $50,000 to $5,000,000. In the case of subscribing to Simplified Value-Prep®, a small monthly subscription gets them into the value-prep game to get ready fast and ready right. There are no barriers of high upfront costs for the owner to digest. By producing operating income, concentrating on cash flow and true value with Simplified Value-Prep®, the owner can build a family legacy, employ others, and earn a living wage plus accumulate long-term business wealth.

MAINTAINING CONTROL AND SECURITY

Owners may not wish to engage an advisor because they do not want to feel incapable or out-of-control. An owner feeling that way is talking with the wrong advisor. While it is natural for an owner to feel some level of embarrassment if their business is having problems, it is not appropriate for an owner to indulge in those feelings by resisting help. Responsible owners have the courage to face the reality they find themselves in and marshal whatever resources are required, including professional advisors.

Advisors can be helpful with an owner's leadership development as well as with the immediate business problem. The right advisor will make their client feel comfortable. They will strive to identify the best in each situation, not just the worst. If an owner senses arrogance, self-interest, or self-righteousness in a potential advisor, that advisor will never pass the owner's sniff test. Resistance to engaging an advisor can be influenced by past experiences, fears of letting go, availability of funds, and a preference for action over reflection. But even in these cases of resistance, I have outlined more reasons and benefits why an advisor may be an excellent addition to an owner's resources.

THE IMPACT OF INERTIA

Many business owners tend to wait too long when they are having a business problem. It may be out of ego or embarrassment. At times, the problem does not hit the owner's radar hard enough, especially if the effects are muted over a prolonged period of time. Sometimes the owner just does not know who to turn to for appropriate advice. Instead, they tend to continue to do what they had been doing before, focusing only on improving execution, hoping that somehow things will go back to the way they were. Few business owners experience crises as opportunities for renewal. That is precisely what crises offer us – a new perspective.

I have worked with business situations described as hopeless, where the owners were afraid of losing everything, including their personal assets. As an objective advisor, I consciously seek, identify, and outline new and creative options that make sense. These are usually options that the owner has been unable to see. I have rarely been in situations where there were not two or three viable options to get out of the crisis situation that the owner has not even considered. Once the owner sees that they have choices, and decides to act, much of the pent-up fear, stress and pain start to go away. The focus shifts from problem to resolution.

I have also advised where the founder became terminally ill in the selling of their business. It was a compassionate and heartfelt journey with the owner and his spouse and it encompassed many levels of preparation. In each critical care engagement, I understand the level of energy and emotion required of caregivers and family members. Having cared for my own daughter during her bout with cancer, I understand firsthand that having an involved party present in these circumstances is essential. The effects of chemotherapy and treatments may affect cognitive abilities and decisions require confirmation by others if they are ill.

Whenever I took on a succession transition or outright sale, I was instantly fully vested as an ally to the owner and their family members. I wanted to include influential spouses who may have been behind the scenes but have a different perspective than the owner's. Even in the worst of times, when fear can be at its highest, there can be a great deal accomplished when high touch connection and positivity are made priorities.

In one of my engagements, a client had a prized hotel franchise that he suddenly was faced with losing. After assessing what the problem was, I met with the staff and told them of the situation. I explained to them I had their interests first in my efforts and that I knew everyone had a family counting on a resolution. I reassured them that I had seen this before, and I honestly told them that there is no guarantee I could do it. But I promised to do my personal best. In return, I needed them to help me and *"take out their lamp from under the bushel basket for all to see"* because it was obvious to our quality scores that we were not communicating how much we cared about our guests.

I described to the employees my personal philosophy of the mind, the hands, and the heart of business. I told them our customers needed to *feel* their care. Their quality scorecard had been languishing. The business was ranked in the bottom 5% for customer satisfaction. I asked them to do one thing for each of the next sixty days—smile. Smile at one another. Smile at the customer. Smile that we had an opportunity to make a change. Smile. Smile. Smile. Look at the guests and smile. It was a straightforward way to relieve the tensions I knew they were feeling and a way for them to positively contribute every day.

The story ends happily. We did get the franchise renewal and we did save the portfolio. We had navigated an almost impossible transition from a point where we were faced with losing the franchise in two weeks. I negotiated an acceptable re-organization and re-license between the Franchisor and the owners. We saved $13 million in the owners' *net portfolio value*. I kept my promise to those employees and the families that relied on this asset for their livelihood. Today they remain as high performers in overall guest satisfaction and brand quality standards. And all of us learned how inertia can be transformed into momentum towards high achievement albeit starting with a smile.

THE IMPACT OF OTHER BLOCKAGES

There are a host of other blockages I can describe that hinder how personal factors work in the business world. They include over-thinking, paralysis by analysis, being stuck in history, a misfit role, obsession with logic, ignoring employees' experiences, a focus only on data, over-rationalizing, and the blame game to name a few. These other blockages yield the same results—an obsession with control, neglect, dereliction of responsibility, lack of accountability, the lack of systems and controls, frustration, and personal depression. As an advisor, we must directly address owner accountability and help reason through these blockages as we seek positive solutions and benefits.

Most times there is an emotional payoff for having a blockage. It may be attention-seeking, control, acting out of anger, aggression, or irresponsibility. One must find the problem beneath the problem to understand the blockage. I have had the occasion to work for or with several personality types that are difficult to make any real progress with on a personal level due to their traits. As is common with any behavior, they exist in shades of gray, but it is worth understanding them:

- **Self-centered** Narcissists - These personality types tend to blame others for what is going on (or not) in the business. There is a pattern of a lack of empathy and or lack of feeling for anyone other than themselves. It is difficult for the self-centered individual to be reflective. Many times, these are very intellectually gifted people. However, their "wiring" may be counter-productive to making any real change.

- **Rollercoaster** Wafflers - These personality types are hot and cold, high and low and may be inconsistent with direction or outright contradictory from one moment to another. It may be difficult to count on these personality types for decision support or to lead a change process. Waffling on decisions to act or not act, to agree or not agree and complaining about it abound.

Trying to understand these two behavioral types may be difficult without the help of a professional in human relations or cognitive psychology. The main point of my short layman's description of personality type behavior above is that you have an awareness of these blockages. They hinder real progress during a transition and impede developmental growth during transformation. The blockages described above make it difficult to develop trust. For advisors, trust is the only bridge to transformation.

THE PARADOX OF OWNER COMFORT

For an owner who typically has up to 85% of their personal wealth invested and locked inside the business, protecting life-long business value has the utmost of significance. An improvement of 1X multiple can mean millions in value. So, what is an owner's payoff for non-action? I see only one answer...comfort. Taking the path of least resistance by working in the business and not on it means the owner is comfortable with the *status quo*.

Comfort also can be cloaked as denial. For those owners mired in denial, no one can help protect them from the consequences of inaction—not even a great and well-intended advisor. Comfort can easily trump any internal efforts to change for the better. It is not unusual to have an owner end up in bank workout after ignoring the basic warning signs of cash flow trouble. Unfortunately, that same owner will pay high bank fees, legal fees, refinancing fees and turnaround expertise to get out of bank difficulties. Many times, the root cause still has not been addressed. Additionally, once out of trouble, there's little incentive for preparation to protect future cash flow and value. They almost have short-term memory loss.

There's also little personal accountability for mismanagement by an owner in a privately held business. It is their time. It is their money. It is their future at stake, and it is theirs for the undoing if they choose. The burden of choice rests solely on their shoulders. From an owner's perspective, a crisis may look like everyday survival, fighting any one of many outside forces beyond their control.

Often, when the business goes haywire, the owner's sphere of influence or lack of systems and controls appear to be the issue. Sometimes that is the case with sudden chance events. As an objective, third-party advisor, you have the benefit of being outside the tornado of events. You can help an owner see what needs to be addressed. Again, their blind spot or bias that manifests in denial will not necessarily be something they are aware of unless they have an astute and truthful advisor.

It is also obvious to many advisors, where there is no accountability, there is usually no work invested to prepare for a constant readiness state. It is akin to denying one's own mortality. These situations may account for up to 80% of the business population. The balance of 20% of owners may actually be uncomfortable in the *status quo*, which motivates them to action. Some may not know why they are feeling unsettled or what to do about it. Some may have been burnt by a quick-fix, sales charlatan and are too cynical or wounded to re-attempt preparation work. Others may keep themselves busy in their comfort zone of operating the business the same way and therefore excuse themselves from pursuing new methods over too much work to do.

All of these situations can be ideal opportunities for you as an advisor. What is most important is you understand what you are seeing and hearing and that you don't accept it at face value. It is much better to apply a line of questioning that peels the onion skin to get to the core of the problem. When you start with the premise that all business owners do not want to suffer unnecessarily, you will be undeterred by these various hurdles presented to take you off course.

CHAPTER FOUR

THE ROLE OF AN ADVISOR

Business advice is something I have engaged, applied, studied, researched, and provided in my career. It is a professional practice that, like other professions, needs to be clearly understood. At times, there may be confusion in the mind of a business owner, as role names can be used interchangeably by many sources.

For clarity, I have outlined the differences I see in the types of roles that may interface with the business owner. These are not the exclusive list of potential roles but are the most common areas we see in the market. Each role below requires a different 'fitness for duty' in order to provide the owner benefit. Understanding these differences helps advisors better define and describe what they do for the owner. The roles we will review are Consultant, Coach, M&A Advisor, and Value Advisor.

As a general outline, it is important to review universal

strengths and weaknesses of any consultant, coach or advisor. We will use the Advisor as an example for all roles.

STRENGTHS OF ANY ADVISOR

An Advisor brings individual strengths to any engagement. Depending upon the assignment and owner expectation, different strengths may be more valuable. Below is a list of potential strengths. An effective advisor:

- Is uncompromisingly confidential
- Is collaborative in style with the owner and other professionals serving the company
- Understands boundaries of their engagement in authority, control and decision-making
- Is a good observer and refrains from making snap interpretations or passing judgment
- Is oriented towards building and earning trust in a relationship
- Communicates clearly, consistently and may over-communicate in times of criticality
- Maintains a respectfully honest approach in determining what the owner wants
- Has a fiduciary duty which includes a duty of loyalty as well as a duty of care that no harm be done to the owner and company. That includes non-competitive assignments
- Has a relationship based on personal respect for the owner and the company, regardless of their

agreement with decisions made by the owner or company's management team

- Has verifiable professional integrity without a hint of reputation risk or impropriety
- Holds objectivity and truth in highest regard when assisting the owner
- Obtains 360-degree input from key team members to utilize as context for recommendations
- From an outsider perspective, has a broad base of experiences that can inform decision making, free of the biases of industry-specific knowledge
- Maintains a deep and broad network of subject-matter experts to tap for solving specific, complex problems, outside the area of their expertise
- Outlines a beginning and an end of service as defined by the scope of work or engagement letter
- Views their role as a teacher, responsible for the education of their clients

There is also a unique phenomenon that may occur during advisory work when introducing new concepts. It may be viewed as both a strength and a weakness. The advisor may unbalance the owner's *status quo,* which the owner may interpret as unsettling or uncomfortable. Psychologists call it educational "confusion."

Emotion, more broadly, plays a vital role in the integration of new knowledge with prior knowledge. Running into problems while learning, an owner may internally be saying, *I do not get it.* That response is often accompanied by emotion, which could include fear, cautiousness, skepticism, brain fade, shutting down, subject jumping, or other avoidance behaviors. Note that this is a normal overwhelm response for any of us during learning, as we struggle with understanding or integrating new knowledge with prior experiences.

These moments are opportunities for the advisor to ease back on the throttle, take a mental break or timeout. With that break, the advisor can restart the topic at hand to allow the owner to catch up in their understanding. Observation therefore is a key advisor strength. Building a feedback loop into the introduction of new topics and learnings is critical so the owner does not mentally and emotionally bail on the critical lessons. This same confusion, if diligently and compassionately addressed, can lead to new and fresh thinking by the owner. Overcoming owner resistance and misunderstanding takes patience. The advisor must be aware of the mindset of the owner during any educational initiative. An advisor therefore must be able to communicate clearly, consistently, over-communicate at times depending upon the criticality of the situation, and be a teacher.

WEAKNESSES OF ANY ADVISOR

An Advisor may bring individual weaknesses to an engagement. One person naturally cannot be expected to address every need of every owner. It is imperative that the advisor recognize when their weaknesses, blind spots, or biases are hindering the progress of an engagement. Here is a list of potential weaknesses. Sometimes an advisor may not:

- Be as sensitive to the owner's temperament as the owner might like
- Bring a needed set of strengths the owner may find helpful
- Build trust or respect which may cause owner resistance and acceptance
- Be able to do it alone and may need an advisory team member present or involved in certain areas to complement a weakness or inexperience
- See key team members clam up or mislead when the advisor is not trusted
- Speak truthfully about the reality of the owner's situation in the hopes of obtaining an engagement
- Be diplomatic or compassionate when they 'go ugly early' in assessing the owner's situation
- Give credit for all the work done by the owner or their team members and may want to take all the accolades
- Have the appropriate experience or knowledge and can only provide general input
- Treat the owner's decisions with respect for their perspective

Having looked at the strengths and weaknesses of any advisor, let us move on to understanding the differences between the distinct roles: Consultant, Coach, M&A Advisor and Value Advisor.

THE CONSULTANT ROLE

A consultant provides a level of in-depth expertise and/or operating knowledge as a subject-matter expert in a way not currently available inside the organization. Tax consultants, technology consultants, organizational development consultants, human resource, lean, engineering, manufacturing, and supply chain consultants are a few examples. Consultants can be found in every area of business where owners may need assistance. Consultants are typically specialists, not generalists.

Most businesses do not have expert resources in their ranks to implement a project without help. As many owners will tell you, a project can fail quickly when trying to implement one alone or without the necessary qualifications. While consultants make recommendations within their functional areas of expertise, consultants are normally not able to assist the owner to implement their recommendations. The owner is called a sponsor of the project, meaning they economically 'sponsor' and support the consultant's activities in the business to make change.

Simplified Value-Prep® and the COACH Method™ are not consulting tools as they do not require a consultant to utilize them. *They are designed as financial tools to lend decision support to a business owner.*

THE BUSINESS COACH ROLE

A business coach typically works to improve the general skills and business acumen of the owner, rather than to address one or more specific issue areas. Therefore, one can find leadership coaches, public speaking coaches, life coaches, and general business coaches. What makes a business coach different from a consultant? The difference is in their approach. A business coach takes the approach of improving the leader of the business. A business consultant takes a more specialized firsthand approach, providing specific solutions for the business itself.

Additionally, cultural development and assembling the right team members with the right strengths is a valuable coaching role. There are many books and assessments available for understanding individual strengths. What comes to mind is the Kolbe Indexes for natural abilities and instinctual strengths by Kathy Kolbe (www.kolbe.com) and the Gallup StrengthsFinder (www.strengthsfinder.com) based on work by Marcus Buckingham & Donald O. Clifton, Ph.D. Coaching a non-performing or average team to high performance is beneficial. A coach has capabilities to influence the team members, but without the authority to hire and fire.

Overall, the business coach works closely with a business owner to mentor and educate one-on-one. Business coaching is more beneficial than self-development, as a coach holds the owner accountable, whereas in self-development, the owner has difficulty maintaining perspective for goal-attainment or accountability.

THE M&A ADVISOR'S ROLE

The M&A Advisor is someone who looks holistically at the big picture surrounding a specific business metric – Fair Market Value and selling price. Their objective is to shepherd a client through the complexities of a sale or purchase and get them to a closing on a transaction.

The M&A Advisor is engaged to prepare, package, and market the owner's business, if it is a sell-side engagement. If it is a buy-side engagement the M&A Advisor seeks qualified target companies for sale that may be a strategic fit for the client and in the case of a buy-side engagement, analyzes the value of the target company and manages due diligence.

The most skilled M&A Advisors are relationship driven. They are oriented towards doing what is in the best interests of the client and their business. That also includes applying a broad and deep knowledge of transactional processes and pitfalls. The M&A role requires extensive education, certification, deal experience, market research, and analysis of industries and trends. The M&A Advisor has developed, or can bring to the engagement, strong private-equity or strategic buyer relationships. The M&A role requires being an effective orchestra leader, collaborator and facilitator, working closely with other professional advisors serving the owner, such as their CPA, attorney, tax professional, or intellectual property counsel. The M&A Advisor may or may not be a licensed securities representative associated with a broker dealer organization, depending upon the size of deals they represent.

An M&A Advisor must know business in terms of the

current market, strategy, finance, and operations. The M&A Advisor need not be an expert in a niche industry. To be effective, an M&A Advisor must understand different business sectors in order to serve them well, for example, manufacturing, services, technology, distribution, logistics and others as specified in The North American Industry Classification System (NAICS). NAICS is the standard used by Federal statistical agencies in classifying business establishments.

And finally, the M&A Advisor must be disciplined to follow a process, using proven methodologies that result in a higher predictable outcome for a transaction. M&A is the setting for where Simplified Value-Prep® and the COACH Method™ were developed, to assist business owners with maximizing the value of their business upon a sale. It is also where the role of Value Advisor was developed.

THE VALUE ADVISOR'S ROLE

Advisors are professionals specializing in asking key questions to assist the owner to understand what they may want and need for the business. A Value Advisor is no different, but they have a specific objective – to maximize the value of the business for the shareholders, partners,or members.

The Value Advisor works in concert with expert evaluators to understand the Fair Market Value of the business for the specific purpose of strategic planning and business preparation. For instance, Simplified Value-Prep® is the tool designed for Value Advisors to assist business owners in maximizing their value. In the process called the COACH

Method™ (Calculate, Orient, Adapt and CHoose) a Value Advisor guides an owner through establishing a Fair Market Value and then ensures that a true value is represented. True value includes the oftentimes overlooked hidden value in the business in intangibles, and off-balance-sheet value that the owner has built. Additionally, the Value Advisor adds a layer of value protection by regularly updating the owner's business value. That routine provides instant access to most current value with any sudden, chance event that may occur during the life of the business.

A Value Advisor is a new advisory role that is in demand due to the negative consequences experienced by the coronavirus pandemic. A Value Advisor has one goal: to maximize the value of the business and prepare it as a decision support tool for an owner to use for the life of the business. You may have heard the adage, *from chaos comes order*. It may be relevant here, as a backdrop to value-prepping a business. It is the Value Advisor's use of tools like Simplified Value-Prep® and the COACH Method™ to balance the chaos of unforeseen events and to apply order to organizing business value. That action thwarts or minimizes the negative consequences of a sudden chance event. The desired outcome is for the business owner to have options and contingencies in times of personal, economic or industry distress.

The Value Advisor may have a background in any number of professions such as a Wealth Advisor, Certified Financial Planner, M&A Advisor, attorney, CPA, Exit Planning Advisor, Corporate Financial Consultant, Organizational Development Consultant or Business Coach. To that end, their understanding of Simplified Value-Prep® and its associated COACH Method™ is their tool to apply for owner decision support to find, build, and protect the true value of the business. Knowing that a Value Advisor has been certified in the application of the Simplified Value-Prep® tool provides confidence and reassurance to a business owner that they are working with a Value professional. That is one of the goals of *The Advisor's Guide to Business Wealth.*

CHAPTER FIVE

SUPPORTING STRATEGIC DECISIONS

Every owner has a dream for their business. It is created by the owner's vision—the guiding north star for the entire organization to follow. Strategy is the plan of action that converts vision to tactics, the actionable steps on the path to fulfilling the owner's vision. Tactics therefore are specific in nature. They are conscious choices made towards a desired outcome. An owner may think they know the business' true value. Usually, that is not the case. If one detail is missed that throws off the business' value, it can derail the owner's next visionary steps. That leaves the owner where they started. And there are A LOT of things that can get missed!

How well internal tactical steps are executed determines the degree to which the organization's overall strategy unfolds. One decision which misses one detail and relies on bad information will lead to negative unintended consequences. There are many outside forces at work that can obstruct or redirect strategy. Sudden chance events can create crises or opportunities. Unforeseen events may have either a positive or negative effect. When the effects are positive, it is described as good fortune or luck. When the effects are negative it is defined as a potential crisis or catastrophe. Chance events then are pivot points of opportunity or threat for the organization.

Therefore, it is important to clarify the owner's vision before validating the true value of the business. Let us look deeper into the Vision Setting process.

THE OWNERS' VISION

Most companies fail to grow not because of product or management issues, but because they continue to do what they have always done to be successful and fail to appreciate the new opportunities and changes the marketplace may be presenting. An owner's vision is therefore evergreen and under influence of internal and external factors. A Value Advisor with diverse operating experience can provide a deep appreciation for the rapid evolution of today's business environment. In fact, cross-industry experience enables a skilled Value Advisor to help the owner identify and evaluate previously unrecognized growth opportunities and develop effective strategies for capitalizing on them.

By working closely with the owner, a Value Advisor may be able to offer new and profitable perspectives for products, services, or lines of business for the owner to consider. There may also be niche' markets, international demand, and potential supply chain consolidations that are available. This is where an owner's vision can be shaped into a carefully prepared strategic plan aligned with calculated risk.

There may also be time considerations that impact the owner's vision. Organic growth may mean slugging it out in the marketplace, which can be slow. Diversifying or acquiring a strategic target may be more advantageous overall, even though it may be a larger, up-front risk of capital investment. These and other considerations for implementing an owner's vision require preparation. A written, well-defined, and executable plan is required for flawless execution. The Value Advisor may help review, edit, or proof the owner's strategy. Transforming owner vision to an operating reality with increasing value is where Simplified Value-Prep® shines and provides multiples of return on the investment of preparation.

With any strategic decision, you will find anticipated and unanticipated consequences. Digressing from the topic of owner vision for a moment, we can learn what sociology tells us about the consequences of owner decisions.

THE LAW OF UNINTENDED CONSEQUENCES

As a backdrop to this chapter on strategy and decision support, I would be remiss without noting the work of Robert K. Merton, considered one of the founding fathers of modern sociology. Merton was responsible for many sociological ideas captured in phrases that became widely used in ordinary conversation, including the "Law of Unanticipated

Consequences," "self-fulfilling prophecy", and its opposite, the "self-defeating prophecy," also known as the "prophet's dilemma."

Much of Merton's analytic work focused on consequences of action that were not anticipated by the actor. Merton, in the mid-20th century, systematically analyzed and classified types and determinants of unanticipated consequences of purposive action. There are positive unanticipated benefits, which we have seen repeatedly as part of serendipity, or serendipitous discoveries in science; there's Murphy's Law type unanticipated consequences: "What Can Go Wrong, Will Go Wrong;" and there are perverse effects that result in the opposite of what was intended.

Merton identified five principle causes of unanticipated consequences: ignorance, error, immediate interest which neglects consideration of longer term and potentially negative consequences, basic values that may enjoin us not to act in certain ways, despite the likelihood of the actions producing unanticipated negative consequences; and self-defeating prophecy in which people do not take action, because they fear negative and unanticipated consequences (also known as the prophet's dilemma). Part of the business ownership experience then is to "expect unexpected events."

As you can see by the sociological impacts of purposeful actions above, decision support tools like Simplified Value-Prep® help us evaluate potential consequences. The goal is to make the right decision by knowing the right information, especially when BIG strategic moves are being considered. Ideally, we want to maximize opportunity and mitigate risk when implementing any strategy. That takes an AIM, READY, FIRE approach to validating value in a seamless platform for value protection, speed, and control.

As we dig further into each potential strategy below, consider the work of Robert K. Merton and why using a decision support tool like Simplified Value-Prep® is extremely helpful to a business owner client.

RENEWING A BUSINESS TO REBUILD

Getting unstuck takes art and science. Many times, routines and old habits reign, people remain unchallenged, comfort remains the goal, and business progress stagnates. A state of inertia drags the business slowly down a path of difficulty on the road to nowhere. A business the owner once dreamed of as a goose laying golden eggs, becomes a golden noose.

If the business has investors or if there is debt in the business, bankers and workout specialists know when it is time for a change. It could be leadership, management, strategy or both. The plan of renewal is to rapidly transform a flailing business from non-profitable to profitable. Usually, a turnaround specialist can help guide the owner to making the necessary decisions to renew the business and return it to normalcy. It is always a painful education for the owner to make these necessary internal and sometimes personal changes. It is a classic case of getting comfortable with being uncomfortable as people, systems and behaviors must change to get the business to turn profitable.

From time-to-time owners may come upon a strategic

opportunity to acquire a business that is spinning its wheels, and where the owner just wants to offload the work involved. There is a method to renew vitality in a business by creating momentum for change and progress. If applied wisely, it can yield significant value to new owners. Many astute organizations seek businesses with poor management. One in particular is a national private REIT for hotels in which I am invested from my family office days. They have a strategic renewal, cookie-cutter process in place ready for management to execute day one of new ownership to maximize true value of the acquisition.

Renewal then is all about building momentum and new direction. In turnarounds, it is called the "Hockey Stick effect." Progression at first is flat, and even may be characterized by a sharp dip, but soon after, it shows a meteoric rise resembling a hockey stick. A Value Advisor knows that executing a vision takes methodical preparation. Knowing and predicting next steps takes a valid assessment and a keen sense of timing along with an understanding of human behavior and motivation.

Being prepared to execute a change provides confidence during times of transformation. Simplified Value-Prep® can support internal renewal efforts. An advisor may be the outside influence that is needed to help the owner get traction driving towards a new vision for the organization.

BUYING A BUSINESS TO EXPAND

An acquisition of a target company may make sense for strategic growth. We know that organic growth takes time, and there is a potential for losing strategic opportunity. If invested capital yields more rapid growth from purchasing a like-company, applying the same invested capital as organic growth, an acquisition makes sense to pursue. Acquisitions also may yield side benefits of valuable personnel, filling gaps in existing capabilities, expanding products or services through diversification, innovative technologies, a new combined and stronger customer base, and operating economies of scale. Acquisitions likewise may bring unforeseen risks as assets may not end up being as claimed, and cultural differences may override operating economies. To that end, engaging a M&A Advisor for target pursuit and due diligence on a buy-side engagement makes sense.

It also may take heavy financial analysis to uncover potential acquisition risks and rewards. That is where an M&A Advisor may be an ideal asset to the owner who may have a bundle of capital, but limited buying experience or personnel resources to draw upon in working through "what if" scenarios. Skilled at listening, asking the right questions, financial analysis, option models, forecasting, data research, and market research, a M&A Advisor offers the owner an independent view. The key value in strategic acquisition is to be able to integrate the opportunity and mitigate its assimilated risks. By having an M&A Advisor perform the analysis, the owner is likely to get an objective and frank perspective.

Internal bias may miss certain deal points or value points altogether.

And when it comes to negotiating an acquisition, the owner may be well served by an external, independent advisor who can assist in evaluating offers, responses, and agreements. Acquisitions take time and may take on a life of their own. They can distract an owner from day-to-day management and therefore cause negative impacts on cash flow and value. If not led by a seasoned negotiator and transaction-savvy professional who knows the potential pitfalls on the path, the acquisition process can be filled with complexities and costs.

Additionally, an owner may lose sight of the initial reason for the acquisition and become too obsessed with the hunt, losing perspective. For these reasons, an advisor may serve the owner as a skilled intermediary who can advance the acquisition process methodically, vet the potential targets efficiently, and provide the owner with an objective, emotional buffer. The acquisition needs to be underwritten by evaluating the true value of the purchaser AND the true value of the target company. This is an ideal environment for Simplified Value-Prep® as a tool.

HOLDING AND BUILDING A BUSINESS

Most business owners would like to see their creations endure. It makes me smile to know my first business is still operating. It is also nice to know that your retirement is provided for and that your family will have a source of passive income for years to come. This goal seems easy but is often difficult to attain without extensive succession planning. The first step is to develop succession plans for both the management and the ownership of the business. If the business is to endure, it must remain in the hands of people who will take care of it and are educated and competent to do so.

The second step is estate planning. Many of our most difficult business advisory engagements involved feuds among heirs. Had I not been involved as an intermediary, much of one estate would have been wasted fighting inter-family legal battles to prove a point, and the company would have been irreparably damaged. Also, no qualified, third-party buyer wants to acquire a company when there is even a hint of litigation.

Diversification of a business is another way for the owner to offset risk. It is no different with professionally managed financial portfolios. Over-concentration on specific customers, product lines, or services can be devastating when major change takes place, especially if it is sudden and out of the owner's control. However, diversification also inherently carries with it a certain level of risk and needs close evaluation, monitoring and analysis.

By performing a product and marketing assessment there may be potential for diversifying products and services within the existing client base. Or there may be justification for diversifying product lines or services based on market demand. A SWOT Analysis is commonly used to address the Strengths, Weaknesses, Opportunities, and Threats of a business and can be applied to uniquely positioning a product or service offering. An owner may want to be on the lookout for these potential opportunities and, before investing time, energy, and capital, perform this internal analysis with the help of an advisor. There have been many businesses that started with one product line and then successfully diversified into multiple product lines to allay the fears of investors. The insight that can be gained before investing is worth the potential disappointment of a failed experiment that has the potential to chip away at or capsize the core business.

In all of the scenarios above Simplified Value-Prep® becomes an internal guidance system for an owner's vision to strategically build their business.

SELLING A BUSINESS TO EXIT

If there are partners or investors involved, making explicit the plan to sell can be critical. Some of the most difficult advisory engagements I have had involved partners who had conflicting expectations about how and when they were going to exit the company, much less how much they were going to be paid for their shares. It is best when everyone agrees and there are few surprises down the road when one party wants to leave or sell, but the other party does not.

Selling the company usually requires significant rethinking for most business owners. Their company is their "baby." Significant parts of their self-esteem are tied up in how successful the company has been and what kind of reputation it has. In other words, the company usually has great intrinsic as well as extrinsic value to its owner. Unless the company is being sold to a relative or an insider who has been intimately involved during much of the company's development, an outside purchaser will not care how much the owner loves it. Potential purchasers will look at the company through their own lens, not the owner's. Any company is only worth what someone else is willing to pay for it.

Think of a company as a product. To begin, develop a marketing plan for the company. What would be of value to others? What types of buyers would be interested? Some buyers might want to keep running the firm as it is, while others might just be interested in key assets (e.g., technology, customer base, physical plant). The process of selling a company can be complex and frustrating. It is always emotional for the owner and often unsettling for the employees. At this point, I have three important suggestions for owners:

- Stay undistracted and continue to focus on building value by using external advisors
- Keep meticulous records and use Simplified Value-Prep® to organize the business and determine its true value
- Engage professionals to advise the owner in the strategic creation and execution process

This is the really hard part in business because there is a build-up of emotional investment after many years of sweat. In my experience, only a small percentage of business owners plan for their exit from the business. Even after a lifetime of arduous work, sacrifice, and investment, very few owners prepare for their biggest payday.

Business schools and entrepreneurial programs seldom discuss the complexities, the costs, or the legalities of an exit. This is a major body of knowledge which impacts business value, and what is eventually left for the owner to invest or spend once the business sale is consummated. There are, however, plenty of business attorneys, business brokers, and consultants standing ready to help the moment an owner has decided to exit. Again, an unprepared attempt to exit a business tends to happen as a last resort. It usually happens after problems have arisen and the value of the business has declined. Circumstances are not ideal, and the owner may be forced to think in terms of scarcity rather than abundance. Taking the business to market under these conditions usually does not command or yield the highest price.

I recommend owners engage a Value Advisor as soon as they start *considering* their exit strategy 1-3 years ahead of the time they want to pull the trigger on the strategy. That Value Advisor (who may also be the M&A Advisor when the time comes to sell) should:

- Be skilled in the confidential marketing, packaging and selling of like-sized businesses.
- Understand the true value of the business using Simplified Value-Prep® to be ready fast and ready right for the market to obtain maximum value.

- Be experienced at leading negotiations and successfully closing deals.
- Know how to solicit, identify, and qualify strategic or private equity buyers who can actually pull the trigger on the sale.

There's anecdotal evidence that engaging a professional Value Advisor yields at least a 20% higher enterprise value for the business owner in the transaction. Selling the business can utilize the preparation and readiness benefits of Simplified Value-Prep®.

SUCCESSION & TRANSITIONING THE BUSINESS

I recommend to business owners that they should decide on their succession goals early to affect a smooth transition, because this decision will impact decision making over the entire life of the company. Succession in a multi-generational, family business has all kinds of dynamics involved. Foremost is the desire of each generation to lead, and what role they may take in the enterprise. Secondly is the preparation and qualifications of the next generation. Transitioning the business in the handoff from one generation to another is critical. The odds are certainly not in the favor of succeeding generations. The "shirtsleeves to shirtsleeves in three generations" adage, which describes the inability of grandchildren to manage the wealth passed down to them from their grandparents and parents, has hung over the world's highest net-worth families for decades, threatening the continuation of family business legacies.

If the owner desires to pass along the business to future generations, it is never too early to put a succession plan in place. Hopefully, it will never be used in an emergency. The process of hiring, training, and evaluating potential successors can be unbelievably valuable in and of itself to the business. The process not only provides reassurance that the company will continue to be professionally managed if something happens to the founder or leader, but it also encourages them to think about exactly what gaps exist and how they will be backfilled.

Simplified Value-Prep® can manage and organize true value in the business. It can be the central source of true value that allows the owners' value-orientation to cascade their views on value to the entire organization.

DISSOLVING THE BUSINESS

Many business owners are under the mistaken impression that all one has to do is lock the doors, hand over the keys and walk away. Nothing could be further from the truth. Most businesses have legal responsibilities to employees, customers & clients, suppliers, regulatory agencies, and taxing entities. Many of these responsibilities do not disappear, just because the company is no longer in business. In particular, tax liabilities and compliance matters may not even go away in bankruptcy. If the strategic plan is to one day cease operations and simply close the business, it is critical to ensure that legal liabilities are minimized and that contracts cover the owner in case of liabilities.

In this case, Simplified Value-Prep® can assist the owners as a final repository of critical documents and transition points. Many documents need to be held for document retention life cycles according to state and federal standards. To that end, avoiding liability and ensuring compliance is critical. Simplified Value-Prep® can offset those risks.

CHAPTER SIX
WHAT IS IT WORTH?

We have all heard the old saying, "Beauty is in the eye of the beholder." When it comes to business, the same could be said of value. Value is in the eye of the beholder. In business, the "beholders" are your clients, prospects, investors, and buyers. For purposes of this chapter, we will cover growing cash and building value, protecting value, the valuation report and process, finding hidden value, and the enhancements and detractors to true value. Finally, we will close with value killers that owners need to avoid or at least mitigate.

GROW CASH & BUILD VALUE

Today more than ever before, the emphasis in fiscal management is on growing cash flow and building value. Just ask any banker about the importance of debt service coverage ratios! Every stakeholder with a financial interest is wondering how to mitigate risks and improve cash flow.

Business sales and transfers are at a socio-demographic point where there will be fewer and fewer qualified buyers in the future as Baby Boomers seek to transfer $10 trillion in value to subsequent generations of owners in the next 10-12 years. That means only the best-in-class businesses will be attractive to strategic and financial buyers. Sweat equity of the owner will not count for much in the marketplace unless it is backed by a business with recurring revenues and strong cash flow. That is why the single most important financial metric in evaluating the progress of a privately held business is its true value defined by the marketplace as FMV. By identifying those actions that build and drive value, your clients will get a much better return when it is time to exit or transfer their business.

THE VALUATION

Businesses are valued for many reasons. Different purposes for valuation drive different valuation outcomes which result in different values. Therefore, a rose is not just a rose when it comes to valuations. Most often, an owner views a valuation report as just another number on a piece of paper that gets filed with no ancillary benefit. When in fact, a valuation report is the *de facto* starting point for building and protecting value.

Purposes for valuations include shareholder buy/sell agreements, marital divorce, business divorce between shareholders or those holding member interests, minority share valuations, Fair Market Valuations in the open market, and other. You get the point. Purpose drives the end report and numbers. Valuations used with Simplified Value-Prep® and the COACH Method™ are for strategic planning and preparation purposes. Although it is a Fair Market Value approach, our purpose is not taking the business to market, but to determine true value, and use it as a management metric for progress throughout the life of the business.

Advisors may hear an owner's objection to performing a valuation, *"We already had a valuation from so and so and we don't need another one."* Or you may hear, *"We get a valuation every year from our CPA for our buy-sell agreement."* That all may be true. This objection is your opportunity to dig a little further to get the owner to elaborate on the circumstances surrounding the valuation – the purpose to ensure it is valid to use for strategic planning and value-prepping purposes. A valuation for the purpose of selling a minority share is significantly discounted from true value. It is always insightful. Most times, educating the owner on valuation purpose is extremely helpful.

The next most important question to ask is what the owner has done with their valuation now that they have it? Is it in a file somewhere unused and untouched until the next one? Additionally, if the business has not been recently valued for market range value, there are many reasons you will want to suggest it with Simplified Value-Prep®. For instance, attractiveness, performance, and economic conditions may have changed, affecting true value. That is where using this decision support tool starts assisting an owner. As their Value Advisor, it is also a significant differentiator for you in the marketplace.

FINDING HIDDEN VALUE

As the name implies, hidden value can be difficult to find, as it is often understated or missing from a company's balance sheet. As such assets are obscured, they are not simply found by analyzing financial statements or using analysis programs. To uncover hidden values, a Value Advisor must invest time into researching and fully understanding all aspects of a business, especially Intangible Assets.

Intangibles are an asset category that encompasses many of the factors that give a company its edge, or its ability to generate better-than-typical future earnings and can be sources of hidden value. Intangibles include the management team talent, a distribution system, a sales organization, the company's culture, and creative or intellectual property (IP) such as copyrights, patents and trademarks, or other forms of protected IP which are licensed or held by the creator. Technology has disrupted the entire system of wealth creation in business. No longer is business wealth locked up primarily in property, fixtures, plants, and equipment. Wealth is created by a company's ability to create, transfer, assemble, integrate, protect and exploit its knowledge assets. It is the intangible assets that can move a Multiple higher during a valuation.

Chris Snider, CEO of the Exit Planning Institute, an organization that prepares Certified Exit Planning Advisors, outlines four categories of knowledge capital, or intellectual capital, which can exponentially increase a business's brand value:

- **Human Capital:** If all other things are equal, a buyer would be more likely to pay more for a company with a talented, seasoned management team than it would for a new team that is just average.
- **Customer Capital:** If your business has deep, lasting relationships with customers that provide recurring revenue, it is more likely to receive more for the business than one with a high concentration of customers, or with a lot of non-recurring revenue, design-build revenue.
- **Structural Capital:** If the business has operating systems and processes in place to support its customer and human capital, it will provide more value than a firm where talented staff or lucrative customers are likely to walk out the door following a transaction. Systems and processes in this category include transferrable key-employee contracts and contracts with critical customers. This also may include systems to make sure intellectual property ownership is protected or recurring revenue is promoted.
- **Social Capital:** Companies that have a clearly defined culture which causes everyone to work

better as a group will attract more than those without a culture.

One of the reasons assets are hidden is accounting standards that regulate how companies report their assets. One such example is real estate – according to Generally Accepted Accounting Principles (GAAP), companies must list their real estate assets at historical cost, which is the original monetary value of the asset when it was first acquired.

For assets like real estate, their value rises over time, yet the increase is not captured on the company's balance sheet. Also, many other assets may be overlooked when analyzing a company's financials. They can include reserves of natural resources, brand equities, and investments that are off the balance sheet in the intangibles section of the balance sheet.

VALUE DETRACTION

Perception of attractiveness may be a value detractor. Without underlying fact sets, subjectivity is a skeptic's bounty. Subjective value in the mind of an owner may also hinder progress towards verifiable and saleable transfer. Emotional value is difficult for people other than the owner to appreciate or to quantify. Therefore, this emotional attachment can be a major hurdle to overcome. In these cases, I have seen owners clutch what they believe is a prized possession, only to lose it later from limiting their thinking.

In one case, I flew by private jet with a business owner

who thought he was receiving an above-average offer from a prospective strategic buyer who had been courting him. They sent us their private Gulfstream jet for pickup. After two hours of meetings, I could see the owner was upset and angered by the purchaser's offer. I asked our hosts if we could take a break, and I suggested a walk outside to my client. We walked and talked for 20 minutes to discuss his response and views on the deal. The owner had had his mind set on a number three times the purchaser's offer. I realized that no amount of discussion would help close that gap. The strategic purchaser had included a build-it-themselves analysis, should they not do the acquisition. But it was flawed and did not include the manufacturing certifications and industry-related experience the owner had built over 25 years. In my mind, true value was somewhere in between the proposal and the owner's view. When we returned from our break, I asked the owner to allow me to lead the conversation and we respect-fully declined any further discussions due to the value gap.

So, who was right on the value of his business, the owner or the purchaser? My point here is that owner subjectivity became a detractor of value. He believed what he wanted to believe was his value. The apparent value gap was something we had pointed out 6 months earlier, but he was firm in his value expectations. We did not engage in a sell-side engage-ment to go to market for that very reason. The fixed value in the owner's mind would eventually lead to a paralysis of never accepting a valid purchase price. Unfortunately, in hindsight that same owner went through bankruptcy five years later when that industry had a downturn and he lost his business.

Haste is a factor that detracts from value. Being pressured by internal or external factors creates an environment of value vulnerability and a buyer perception that the owner will take any offer. So, taking time to prepare true value has the benefit of withstanding other pressures.

Obviously, objective factors can lead to reductions in value. Cash flow constraints, inability to service debt using traditional banking debt coverage ratios, key employee resignations, high inventories, poor accounting, unassignable contracts, undocumented processes, high costs and low gross profit, customer deposit liabilities, compilations versus review statements or audits, off-balance-sheet loans, any appearance of being shrewd, cagey, or disreputable, and changing one's mind constantly after agreeing are some common factors. There are many, many, more objective factors that need to be vetted during analysis.

VALUE ENHANCEMENTS

Scott Bushkie, CEO of the global Cornerstone International Alliance of M&A Advisors in his book *Finish Strong: Sell Your Business on Your Terms (Amazon, 2021)* suggests ways to enhance a business' value before selling. Scott provides in-depth descriptions of several of these value-enhancing factors. I am adding other factors from my own M&A experiences to his list in the bullets below:

- Being organized and having clean accounting
- Financial Audits are the highest level of buyer-acceptable financial results and typically with less associated due diligence
- Independent Quality of Earnings (QoE) reports to prove out cash flow
- Management Team in place that is seasoned and can function owner-independently
- Driving cash to the bottom line
- Reducing debt and liabilities, and appropriately managing Accounts Payables and Accounts Receivables
- Reducing working capital needs in the business
- Increasing turns in inventory and housekeeping of older or unsaleable inventory
- Non-competes in place for key employees
- Transferable and assignable customer agreements in place
- Recurring revenue based on longer-term agreements
- Documented processes and systems that control throughputs and actions
- Culture that fits with a potential strategic or private-equity purchaser
- Appropriately re-casted financial statements including P&L and Balance Sheet
- Realistic forecasted P&L and Balance Sheet for 3-5 years
- Consistency of applied accounting standards;

addressing tax items such as interstate or internet-based sales tax nexus

- Diversification of customer, services, products, or lines of complimentary business
- Growth history and growth potential in the market sector
- Attractiveness of the business as an investment for growth and value appreciation
- Business type of B2B, B2C, B2BC that fits the private-equity or strategic purchaser
- Business process automation that may provide a proprietary or dominant competitive edge
- Ability to grow the business, diversify it and de-risk, gain economies of scale, and market leadership

As you can see, opportunities abound to find value enhancements. Likewise, these factors can be built into the Value-Prepping process to measure true value growth and value appreciations. Simplified Value-Prep® and its COACH Method™ addresses these value drivers and enhancements to maximize the true value of your client's business.

VALUE AS A STRATEGY

Strategy is the plan of action of the business. Using value as a strategy means that it becomes the one metric to assess progress towards building business wealth. Establishing clear and agreed upon expectations and then measuring results against those performance measures determines progress. Periodic review of value is core to the success of an advisory relationship. Expectations, metrics, and commitment should be set early and revisited often as progress is made or the business' situation changes.

Clear accountability can be difficult in advisory relationships. While gathering information, outlining potential options, and making recommendations are the responsibilities of the advisor, it is the owner who makes the final decision and makes resources available for implementation. Owners do not always do what advisors recommend, nor are they always willing to invest the resources required. So, progress variability exists in owner execution.

The simple 3-step approach to finding, building and protecting true value in a Value Advisory relationship is easily described as: AIM, READY, FIRE. These three steps lay out clearly the intent of each party and the expected outcomes. Each party only needs to accept and fulfill their role in the process. Here is a simple diagram of the Simplified Value-Prep® Process from an Advisor and Owner perspective:

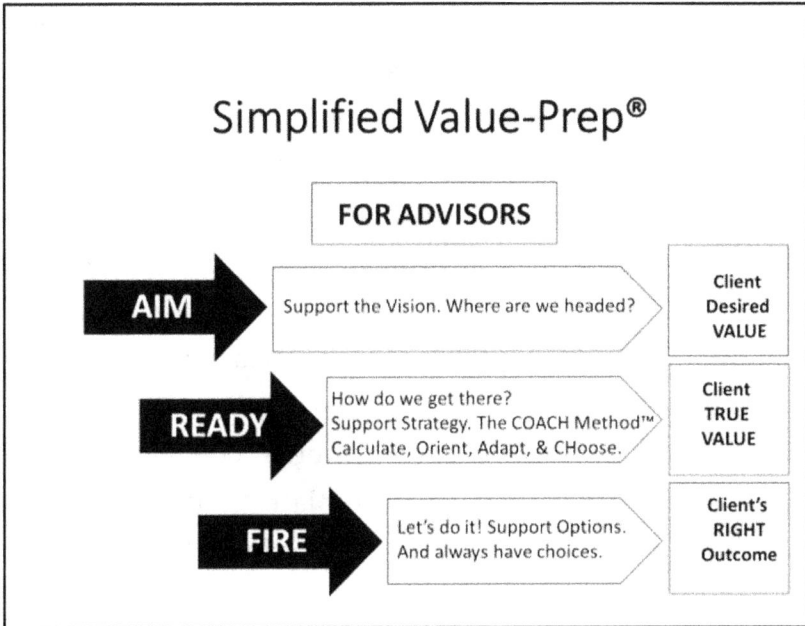

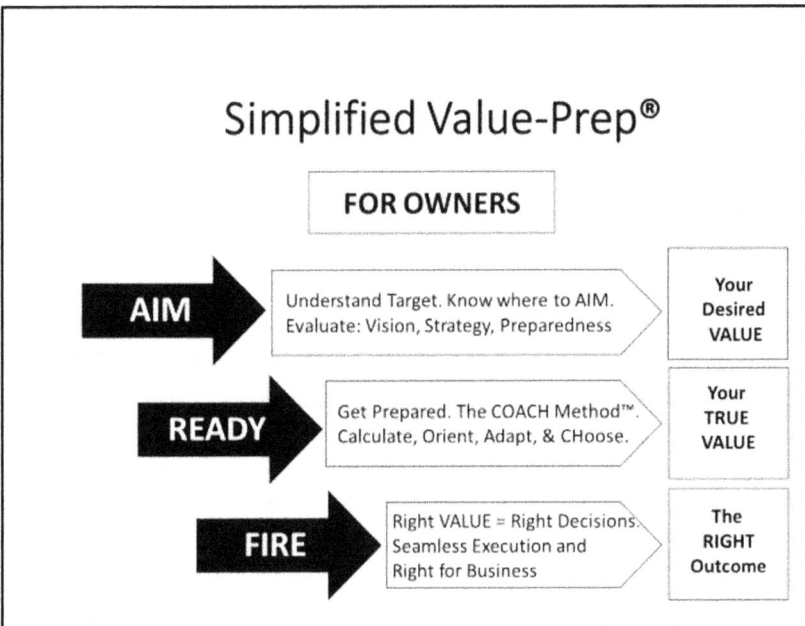

Naturally, specific metrics and their interpretations will change from business to business. Each owner may have a way to measure verifiable progress in their industry. Many industries have related Associations that offer *State of the Union* industry reports. They also may compile and compare historical financial results of member companies organized by upper, middle, or lower results. The reports may include sharing best practices to help improve member performance, another valuable benefit to association membership. Measuring progress therefore is not a new concept and owners may already have them in place for their own business. Here are a half dozen effective metric qualities:

1. Easily understood by the organization, clear and objectively measurable.
2. Focuses on the problem or opportunity at hand, rather than on individual contributions.
3. Reflects the vision of the owner and monitors the execution of strategy as periodic progress updates.
4. Includes opportunity costs and the risks of NOT acting.
5. Evolves as the owner builds trust with an advisor and learns new ways of evaluating progress in the business.
6. Measures ROI, whenever possible, including business advice as an investment, not an expense.

Simplified Value-Prep® uses its universal, 3-step approach to finding, building and protecting true value. By assessing owner VISION, aligning it with Strategy and level of Preparedness, it prepares the business using the COACH Method™ to define the business' True Value. It is up to the owner to then EXECUTE and obtain the RIGHT OUTCOME using the tools provided.

VALUE PROTECTION

In business, there is this false belief when times are good that things will always remain the same. Consider the historic recessionary downturns we discussed earlier. After 10 years of economic expansion between March 1991 and March 2001 we experienced a recession after the tragic 9/11 event. During the same time from 1995 to 2000 was the dot-com bubble which burst in 2002. Then in 2007-2009 we experienced the Great Recession from the mortgage crisis. Was the 20-year mark of positive returns in mid-2021 the telltale timeframe predictor for a recession? The Coronavirus Pandemic has certainly stressed our supply chain constraints, which have not rebounded. If there is one thing we count on, change is constant. We need to be more prepared than never before to ride through changing tides. Will inflation drive a new recessionary period? Or will billions in cryptocurrency value disappear overnight preceding the next economic crash? The point here is, we need to prepare our business to withstand these potential economic tornadoes. Simplified Value-Prep® and the COACH Method™ is one method to doing so.

Since the onset of the pandemic, everyone looking at economic tea leaves is wondering when will the good times return? Some believe the fundamentals are good for prospering. While others are holding their breath anticipating the next major recession around the bend. Regardless of which camp you are in, recession pessimist or recession optimist, being in a constant business readiness state affords an owner a blanket of protection.

The pertinent questions are, *what can we be doing as advisors to influence business value and positively impact the business owner's legacy and family? What can we do to address this apparent opportunity to be constantly ready, to save jobs, impact employee families and leave a wealth legacy? What can we do to offset sudden events and insulate the business value an owner has so tediously built over a lifetime of work?* The answer is adopting an attitude of business readiness. That is where Simplified Value-Prep® is a viable solution for every business owner.

THE SELF-INSURANCE BENEFIT

I often allude to business preparation and the resultant readiness state as "self-insurance." It is a paradox that owners will pay for general, property, casualty, EPLI, medical, life, and disability insurance premiums throughout the lifetime of their business, for any number of potential causes that may never happen. Yet, many owners resist taking action to prepare their businesses to insulate and protect their business' true value. Here are some points to consider:

- There is an iron-clad, 100% guarantee every

business will transition at some point in its
lifecycle.

- The odds of a successful economic outcome are
dismal and not in the owner's favor. Only one-third
of the businesses that go to market eventually sell.

With those odds stacked against them for a successful
outcome, owners remain comfortably in denial of business
readiness preparation. This is what makes this work of business readiness challenging as an educational objective.

Business transitions are something we must deal with as
business owners. If ignored, value will be lost. Transitions can
be opportunities to flourish if a business is appropriately
value-prepped. The business may be transitioned to unrelated third parties such as individual buyers, private equity,
or corporate strategic buyers. It may be transferred to family
members or insider management teams. Or it may transition
as a liquidation, bankruptcy or Article 9. With that 100%
guarantee in mind, the question remains, *"What business
owner wouldn't want control of their transition?"* That is where
Simplified Value-Prep® shines as a decision support tool. It
smooths the effects of change or "transitions points" in business. It is designed from a true value perspective and with the
owner in mind. Its application has provided many valuable
lessons: managing and mitigating risk, as well as building
and protecting value using the combined power of collaborating with other key professionals.

Planned and unplanned business transitions have the
potential to significantly impact business owners, their fami-

lies, their ongoing livelihoods, employees who trust and believe in them, and the overall value of their businesses. Securing an economic future by owning a business means living with and adapting to the demands and risks of business transitions. When Simplified Value-Prep® is initiated, the readiness process is in place to provide owner decision support for any transition caused by choice or chance events.

VALUE KILLERS

Unplanned crises impact business owners' wealth-building efforts. Procrastinators say they will get around to it and may decide, *it is better to be lucky than to be good.* Their justification prevails for not preparing because they may be uneducated or unscathed. Risk takers by nature, owners and entrepreneurs may not heed words of caution you or I provide. Unfortunately for them, it may become too late to make this critical decision once a crisis occurs.

As for naysayers and non-believers alike, I have seen case after case where this one decision not to value-prep determined the difference between an abundant or meager future. Fifty percent of business owners will involuntarily sell or transfer a business because of a sudden event thrust upon them (death, divorce, disability, distress, or disagreement). For all we do control, this one decision to value-prep influences the amount of wealth they have worked so hard to build in their business.

The biggest value-killing threats may be owner ignorance, fear, comfort or just living in the present and missing signs of trouble ahead. A lack of visibility contributes to this justification. There are no guarantees that any business will survive a catastrophic event. But if we want to protect our investment, Simplified Value-Prep® offers an owner a method to thwart or minimize the damaging effects of sudden chance events, as opposed to being unprepared altogether. We cannot protect ourselves from every potential catastrophe and are not suggesting that as a daily frame of reference. What we are recommending is that preparation provides reasonable options and contingencies *in the event of an unplanned, sudden chance event*. In that light, by having done the preparation work to find and build true value in the business, we naturally consider choices we may have when faced with a crisis.

Experiencing rapid loss from risks in a brief period of time is not specific to a private company. In his 2014 article, Dr. Ajit Kambil, Global Research Director, CFO Program at Deloitte LLP revisited an original Deloitte research, *Disarming the Value-Killers: A Risk Management Study*, Deloitte (2005). He and his colleagues found many public companies that lost 20 percent or greater in value within a one-month period, relative to a broad market index. They outlined the underlying drivers of rapid, value-reduction and identified four broad categories of risk contributing to company value-killers, which are represented below.

Strategic risks	Financial risks	Operational risks	External Risks
• Demand shortfalls	• Poor financial strategies	• Earnings shortfall	• Declining commodity prices
• Customer losses/problems	• Asset losses	• Cost overruns	• Rating impacts
• Pricing pressures	• Goodwill & amortization	• Poor operating controls	• Industry crises
• Product/services competition	• Liquidity crises	• Accounting problems	• Legal risks
• Product problems	• High debt and interest rates	• Capacity problems	• Country economic risks
• Regulation		• Supply-chain issues	• Weather losses
• R&D		• Employee issues and fraud	• Partner losses
• Management change		• Noncompliance	• Political issues
• Corporate governance		• High input costs	• Terrorism
• Miscommunication/false guidance		• IT security	• Foreign Economic issues
		• Supplier losses	

Exhibit 4. from *Disarming the Value-Killers: A Risk Management Study*, Deloitte (2005)

Although Dr. Kambil researched public company drivers, one can easily see how a corresponding private company can be negatively affected by any one of these value-killers. Unforeseen events that are value-killers then are not so uncommon as we might think. Had Dr. Kambil revisited this list in 2022, he would have added Global Pandemic as an External Risk. We certainly would from our experience! Value killers need to be noted as bellwethers for using a process with value-protection qualities like Simplified Value-Prep®.

CHAPTER SEVEN

LEADING CHANGE

The business owner must lead any successful business change effort. Here are the effective change management practices I developed and adopted, which were instrumental in making meaningful change possible with my clients:

- **Leading With Heart** – Obtaining minds, hands, *and hearts* of those involved in the change process
- **People First, Always** – Everyone involved needs to understand the potential impact that changes will have on them personally. When secrets are kept by management, workers usually assume the worst and may become actively resistant
- **Relying On Others** – There are always more people involved in any change than there initially appears to be. It is critical to appreciate and leverage that interdependence

- **Relying On Strengths** – Everyone needs to be working with their strengths. In the middle of a critical change process there is no time to correct individual deficiencies
- **Achieving Engagement** – When people are included in the process and understand why things are being done, they become supportive. Otherwise, the best you can hope for is compliance
- **Building Momentum** – People's support is built over time. All initial successes, no matter how small, need to be recognized
- **Measuring Progress** – Step back to measure direction and financial impacts of change

Recognize that Simplified Value Prep® and the COACH Method™ is a driver of change in how an owner and their organization may currently be evaluating business progress. Each one of the above steps has had profound effects on my client's outcomes. The action to ADAPT is a critical component of Simplified Value-Prep® in the COACH Method™.

LEADING WITH HEART

Whenever leading financial change, owners successfully launch change efforts by communicating beliefs and goals to a general assembly. In one case, I had eighty-four people in a distribution and processing business with whom to share my strategy. That business had been floundering under a leader with no previous ownership experience nor any real proof of management leadership. The organization's morale was low and momentum was stalled. The co-founders had retired three years earlier and an internal successor with much industry experience was ordained to lead by the retiring co-founders. The corporate investor though was experiencing a succession plan gone badly with 3 years of significant losses. The new President had produced a downward slide of profits into negative seven figures with piles of excuses.

I accepted this particular assignment knowing that I needed to "raise the bridge and lower the water," at the same time, an unusual two-fold change process. It was required due to industry consolidation, margin compression and an out-of-balance cost structure with route delivery inefficiencies. The situation also required an increase in sales revenue when the industry was trending downward 9% per year. I knew it would be a two-year turn and not an easy transformation.

A few weeks after my initial on-site assessments, I wanted everyone to get the same message at the same time, to grasp the turnaround plan. At the general assembly and with the fervor of a midsummer night's preacher, I called each person to help me in three simple actions that were easy to understand and remember. I told them that in order for change to occur, I wanted *their minds, their hands and their hearts* in the business - every moment, every day. I promised that if we did so as an organization, we could succeed at changing the business. That is when I could feel the energy starting to spark, as people began to identify personally in their own way, with the vision I shared of change and care for their future.

Furthermore, I explained that

- **If we only used our minds**, and did not act with conviction, the changes we wanted to make in the business would not be seen or felt by our customers and we would fail
- **If we only used our hands,** without mind and heart, that we would be the busiest we could ever be. But we would end up on the road to nowhere spinning our wheels
- **If we only used our hands and heart,** but did not engage our minds, using common sense as our compass, we would end up lost again

Most importantly, I outlined that *if we put our hearts into the business*, our minds and hands would follow. We needed to take the risk of doing things differently, experimenting, making mistakes, and potentially looking silly while being vulnerable. By putting ourselves out there for our customers to reconnect, we could reshape the business. If we did this, we would reach our destiny and dreams. By using our minds, hands, and heart, we would take the right actions for the right reasons and would succeed. We would internalize our purpose and mission.

I reinforced my concept—mind, hands and heart—over and over and over again, whenever the opportunity arose. And what do you think started happening? The miracles of change quietly started to appear as individuals and teams worked as collaboratively on solutions while still running their day-to-day duties. Eventually, costs were lowered and sales rose. Margins were preserved, unprofitable customers chose to leave us, and we worked our way out of financial difficulty over twenty-two months. Two years from the start, the business was sold. The successor I had groomed to replace me, who had been overlooked in the original succession plan, navigated the business to the finish line with a profitable sale. I mentored him and saw his potential my first week. He went on to become CFO of a $40 million dollar distribution business that transformed into a $1.3 billion business. His journey is a remarkable success story, and we remain good friends today.

I want to make an important clarification on leading with heart. The minimum acceptable score is three out of three: All three elements, *mind, hands, and heart,* must be engaged before real progress is made in any business. This model of mind, hands, and heart became the legacy from my turnaround work. I have applied it several times thereafter when confronted with adapting to change. By enlisting peoples' minds, hands, *and hearts* I found any transition or transformation in business was possible. To this day I believe deeply in the power of people in my client's organizations to make extraordinary contributions to true value.

PEOPLE FIRST, ALWAYS

People are the primary conduit by which business operates. People are the spirit of the business. People shape culture. People create and follow processes. People innovate or resist.

People show respect and dignity in the workplace or express their personal biases and frustrations. People connect with customers. People ARE our customers. People are the key to business greatness.

I have never seen a business that utilized even a fraction of the intellectual and emotional resources available within its people. Perhaps because it is obvious, too close, or in a blind spot, business owners may fail to utilize people as an available resource for change. In learning organizations, one of the key ingredients is that people have a passion for knowledge, understanding and trying new things—responsible experimentation. Hidden inside people in a business, including the business owner, is a huge untapped potential for problem-solving, innovation, and options. Simplified Value-Prep® is a tool that draws out the best in people when they collaborate as a team for the benefit of the business.

Within every company I have ever worked, there were creative problem-solvers and unconscious option-seekers that the owner never even dreamed of tapping for help. They were right there in the business! The secret is that it costs nothing extra to harness the powerful resources of people already employed. People want to give their personal best and owners desirous of making change need to explore how to mine their value. The message of "people first, always" is to adopt an attitude of abundance as a believer in untapped potential. The people in place can deliver more than one can imagine. Allow them to become a key part of the change process. Owners can then rely on them to help carry the business through any transition or sudden chance event.

RELYING ON OTHERS

Business owners by their very nature do not like to be dependent because of potential vulnerability. Their nature and existence as an owner are due to their self-image or internal needs for self-reliance and independence. That is likely why they started a business in the first place. However, what initiated the start of the business may not help it stay in business. When the business becomes more than one person, expectations change. That can become frustrating, unless an owner understands that being in business means accepting and adopting interdependence. I liken interdependence to a "partnership" between owner and employee.

The concept of interdependence is that one person relies upon the other to fulfill certain commitments. Earlier in the guide I referred to this reliance between advisor and owner as a "duty of care." The same duty of care exists between an owner and their people in holding one another's best interests at heart. The owner and employees are interdependent.

It's been said a thousand times: people are a business' major asset. Living that mission is an owner's role. A job is a person's major asset. Each person depends on the other in important, rich, complicated, and very personal ways. When the owner-employee partnership is based on mutual respect and trust, it flourishes. When either party breaks that trust and acts to take more for themselves at the expense of the other, then the partnership dies, and the business goes with it.

Think about this for a moment. It is very unlikely that an

owner creates a business alone. There usually are explicit or implicit commitments from a lot of other people including:

- Employees
- Lenders
- Investors
- Suppliers
- Partners
- Customers
- Family members

These people are "stakeholders" in the business. They may have given time, money, emotional support, legal commitments, and/or given up other opportunities to work with that owner. Each of these stakeholders relies on the owner to honor their commitments to them. The owner also relies on the stakeholders to fulfill their commitments to the business. Some stakeholders have bet their careers and their family's welfare on the company. This is a big responsibility for the owner.

But stakeholders also have a responsibility to deliver on what is expected of them. The level of this duty of care to one another and reliance of both the owner and the stakeholders on one another grows as the business grows and expands. The benefits of successful change cannot be realized unless an owner and their people understand the concept of interdependence. When the business faces a difficulty, asking for help can be a vulnerable decision for any owner. However, getting everyone engaged is valuable.

Applying common sense to disclosure is appropriate, depending upon the transition at hand. It is also where you as a Value Advisor may become an invaluable resource. When business owners feel the most alone, vulnerable or dependent is generally when they isolate themselves or their thinking and *that limits their potential for options and solutions*. At these moments of turmoil, with pressure mounting, an owner can easily feel overwhelmed. The owner may ruminate and suffer the isolation of that decision to ruminate alone. When the owner can rely on others, inside or outside the business, navigating through their loneliness, much of the personal stress is eased.

Relying on others means when one wins, everyone wins. Viewing the adoption of advice as an interdependent duty of care to one another allows everyone to concentrate on their own role in the transition, providing options, solutions, possibilities, and best efforts at every stage.

RELYING ON STRENGTHS

Relying on strengths means knowing who is capable of doing what in the business. When leading a change effort, I wanted the internal leaders and change agents to work in the areas of their strengths. This will reduce costs, reduce management efforts, reduce error rates, and reduce the time needed for results.

In my early work I relied upon my own assessments of people's strengths using interview techniques and intuition. Later, I found that utilizing a standardized instrument to evaluate strengths was much more efficient and dependable. Additionally, they validated my intuitive insights. I recommend that if your client is contemplating a critical transition, you explore these resources I list below. Strength assessment is a key resource to any business owner where having that knowledge applied can boost business performance. I am sure these are not the only references on strengths available. However, these are two resources I have personally used and have recommended to others to use. They are:

Kolbe.com – And the 35-year work of Kathy Kolbe on conative (instinctual) strengths of the individual and the research of The Center for Conative Abilities. Kolbe provides standardized assessments and an understanding of the natural strengths we are born with to use. (kolbe.com)

Gallup® StrengthsFinder® - Based on study of two million people over a 25-year period identifies the most prevalent human strengths in the Internet-based Strengths-Finder® Profile as more fully described in the book: _NOW, Discover Your Strengths_ by Marcus Buckingham & Donald O. Clifton, Ph.D. (gallupstrengthscenter.com)

Both assessments help to qualify where people may fit best in the business and how people may perform more utilizing their strength potential. For now, the takeaway is: always work on strengths and complement weaknesses.

As Jim Collins book on _Good to Great_ intimates, to go from a good company to a great company you need disciplined people, disciplined thought, and disciplined action. A company is made up of people. It is exponentially more valuable to the business to bring people from good to great than it is to bring them from bad to mediocre, or even from mediocre to good. When adapting to change, people working in areas of their strength build a confidence that is unmatched. You may even find hidden strengths that manifest from adversity. Momentum builds more quickly. Likewise, insights for options, solutions, and possibilities present more quickly.

The next practice is to understand the role of connectedness during the change process in achieving engagement of the entire organization.

ACHIEVING ENGAGEMENT

One book in particular imparts the importance of connection in business quite clearly: *Shine: Using Brain Science to Get the Best from Your People*, by Edward M. Hallowell, M.D. Hallowell states,

"Connection is the most powerful tool we can use to bring out the best in others and ourselves. In contrast, disconnection in the workplace may be the single most preventable, detrimental force that leads to underachievement, depression, disloyalty and job loss."

Connection is the glue that binds people emotionally to their performance. I call this act of connectedness: engagement. When people are *engaged*, they have their minds, hands and hearts in the business and seem to be in a timeless state, focused on the task at hand, no matter how insurmountable it appears. They feel and believe that they are a part of something larger than themselves.

When people are engaged,

- They believe that people they like, and trust are relying on them to come through.
- They believe that someone is looking out for their best interests.
- They produce better results.
- They feel motivated from positive reinforcement for the behavior that is valued.
- When asked to help, or their opinions and input, they feel valued.
- When something good is noticed and communicated, they feel recognized and appreciated.
- They want and respond to consistent, regular feedback, and over-communication.

Engagement is sparked in individuals and groups when their leader believes they can accomplish something big. Many times, it is something to accomplish that has never been done before. It is the positivity report card concept of starting out with an A+ and then working to keep it. Confidence is built when positive contributions are noticed and recognized. Recognition instills a sense of appreciation. I have seen the ordinary line worker transform into an extraordinary contributor during a business crisis based on these practices. Nurturing potential draws out the best in people to achieve extraordinary results. Engagement is an emotional process of getting everyone connected and focused "all-in" during times of business complexity.

It takes an emotional sensitivity and commitment to be

engaged and in the frame of mind of positivity and creativity. As an advisor, I want to surround myself with that "feel good" energy especially in intensely difficult circumstances. In fact, it brings out the best in people and their actions, and it brings out the best in us as advisors. I can find something good in the strengths of any person and in any situation regardless of how dire, and I can find ways to address boundaries and correct behaviors without disrespecting anyone who wishes to remain stuck in negativity.

BUILDING MOMENTUM

It is my observation that every business has a unique collective personality that is formed over time based on mindset and how people in the business feel–what some might call a business culture. I use the term personality in reference to an emotional quality, the essence of a business that one feels the moment you walk into the doors or meet an employee or interact with a customer service representative. If we are open, we can feel that business personality when visiting, working in, or working with a company. We either like it or we don't. Typically the telling exchange is how we are treated as an outsider. That interaction speaks volumes as to what is going on internally within the business. The business' collective personality is an aggregate of the beliefs and emotions of the people associated with a company that shines through to the outside.

On the negative side, a business' personality can manifest itself as a sense of discouragement, even despair, which erodes productivity, and morale. Personality may present as employee resistance, grousing, fearfulness to decide, or apathy. Negative personality traits may be heightened in a downward spiral of the business or crisis when everyone is feeling the intense pressure of difficult financial circumstances. Emotional neural networks can solely drive the bus on decision-making. In negative situations, the emotional reaction is to fight, flee, or freeze.

A business' personality stems from how people are appreciated, how their work is valued, and how that value is communicated to them. A business' personality starts with the owner. It is the owner who sets the pace for beliefs and standards within the organization. It is the owner who communicates responsibly and compassionately. Therein the business owner becomes a teacher in words and in deeds. The business personality is a mirror of the owner and is reinforced each day.

If we are taught to contribute to a safe environment, we will do so. If we are taught to mistrust and be untruthful, we will do so. If the owner is a leader with vision, we will follow. If we know the owner cares about us, we will give our hearts, hands, and minds to our work. And so, it goes. Whatever is practiced by the owner, the employees will practice. It is the emotional flame of passion and purpose that fuels action.

As the sponsor of change, an owner must consider the personality of the business and its emotional energy. Because the collective personality *includes* the owner, and is influenced by the owner, an independent, objective advisor may be better at facilitating the building of momentum. The owner may wish to remain a part of the solution and be perceived by the followers as "the owner" and not necessarily the change agent. The emotional difference as interpreted by their people is: "We are all in this together and it will take all of us to get out of this together," rather than "I'm feeling the pain, so I'm going to spread it around."

Understanding the business' collective personality is critical to building emotional momentum for change and for the adoption of advice. When people feel safe, they respond by investing their minds, hands, *and hearts* in support of the needed changes. The art of transformation is when the business' emotional state changes from victim to victory through leading with heart, accepting interdependence, relying on people and their strengths, achieving "all-in" engagement, and momentum.

MEASURING PROGRESS

The successful adoption of business advice can be measured by observing the quantifiable fiscal impact. A goal is of no use unless the owner has a reliable way of determining whether or not that goal has been achieved. What is first necessary is to set the above practices in motion in a digestible timeline I call chunks. These chunks may also be called milestones, critical tasks, or gates. What is important is to address progress by assessing:

- **Priorities** – Depending upon the positive/negative consequence, which objectives have the most positive/negative impact in a ranked order?

- **Momentum** – Are initial results being achieved rapidly enough to gain internal momentum and build confidence in eventual overall success?
- **Clear Focus** – Are the goals, steps, and metrics of the change effort clear to everyone involved?
- **Flow** – Is progress becoming easier due to momentum, and is any remaining resistance fading?

It is important that everyone involved be able to recognize and appreciate the progress being achieved. Progress needs to be regularly reported to become integrated. Progress cannot be a secret. Making sure that progress can be reached in a reasonable timeframe provides immediate gratification and increases confidence, motivation, and momentum. Consistent communication makes sure that the messages of little victories are spread to encourage others in their engagement. Measuring progress and having a communications feedback loop is where an advisor or internal Project Manager can provide scorecards, news flash reports, or supporting communications to the business members, letting them know how things are going.

ENGAGING STAKEHOLDERS

Not everyone that needs to support the change effort actually works in the business. Customers, suppliers, lenders, and, on occasion, government officials may play critical roles in making required changes. Working with people outside of the company presents certain special challenges. Among these are:

- It is hard to ensure confidentiality
- Outside stakeholders have primary loyalty to themselves and/or their own organizations, not the owner's business
- There is usually little the owner can do to deter non-compliance

I have learned that the following practices work well:

- Gain alignment on the exact nature of the problem. Everyone needs to agree on what is going on, and why
- Find the common ground where goals are shared between the parties
- Always tell the truth. The outside stakeholder must trust both the owner and the advisor
- Present the benefits and costs of the changes from each party's viewpoint. The other party may have to explain the situation to someone else and, therefore, it must make sense from their perspective, too

MAKING ADVICE WORK

Each of the practices I have outlined in this chapter are instrumental in making business transformation possible. As a Value Advisor you do not need to be expert in the above practices. What is more important is that you are aware of practices that have worked from experience so you might identify them at work. Which practices get applied depends upon the complexity of the business circumstances. How accurately these circumstances are recognized depends on a professional assessment of the business and the unique set of conditions it faces. The point is, do not allow the business owner to give up if faced with the need to transform the business. Find the right answers. If you stand by that client in tough times, and have been a help to them, you will have earned a client for life.

To navigate and transcend negative circumstances and sudden negative chance events, a business must adapt to complexity and must change in order to be renewed and revitalized. By engaging others in an interdependent partnership, every person in the business becomes an agent of change. Relying on others' strengths that are oftentimes hidden and untapped is a key to achieving engagement and building the momentum for change. As waves of momentum crest, insights become unforeseen options, solutions and possibilities for the journey towards renewal. My advice to business leaders is this: enlisting a trusted, professional advisor makes the navigation through difficulty a rewarding experience—personally, professionally, and financially.

EPILOGUE
ARE YOU READY TO VALUE ADVISE?

At this point in our journey, it is my hope that you have gained insights from the advisory experiences I have shared, and that in some way, my career's work in Value will help illuminate your advisory path in guiding business owners. What follows in this chapter is a final collection of my thoughts and outlooks on the importance of finding, building, and protecting the true value of a business so that one day, your client business owners may receive a payday of business wealth. These are some reflections you may consider when deciding if Simplified Value-Prep® and the COACH Method™ are right for introduction to your clients. Our story is conveniently located on our website for your clients to consider: www.value-prep.com.

SPEED OF BUSINESS

In an age of speed and technology, business has higher risks to address and manage, especially since the most recent 2020-2022 global pandemic and economic fallout. Like the high-speed flying formation of the *Blue Angels* squadron, foremost in my mind is that at higher and higher speeds, one business indecision or wrong decision can cause a catastrophic crash of a life's work. There is a natural response to a distance runner that occurs when an upper limit is reached: systems tend to collapse. It is no different in business. We need business systems built for speed and sustainability.

Clients get immersed in the "reality" of their situation. As advisors, we have a valuable perspective to share with clients – objectivity and distance. From afar we can see something differently than what an owner may see in the eye of the tornado. As speed is demanded by competition, markets, consumer demand or any other number of drivers, it is more important than ever before to be ready for calamity and opportunity.

BUILDING ON TRUST

An article from the Harvard Business Review has been saved in one of my folders for over 20 years. In it, excerpts are taken from the book, *Management Challenges for the 21st Century*, by Peter F. Drucker. The article is titled *Managing Oneself*. In that article, Drucker points out that over a 50-year working life, one must be able to learn how to manage, develop, and position themselves to make the greatest work-life contribution.

Drucker goes on to support this premise by advocating strengths assessment, working in ways that people best perform, and not trying to force individual change to gain a result. In other words, Drucker suggests the best results come from applying strengths to the requirements of the position to gain high performance.

Drucker goes on to say that in order to manage oneself the key question to ask is: What are my values? It is the foundation of building trust as an advisor in business.

"Organizations are no longer built on force, but on trust. The existence of trust between people does not necessarily mean that they like one another. It means that they understand one another. Taking responsibility for relationships is therefore an absolute necessity. It is a duty. One owes that responsibility to all one's co-workers: those whose work one depends on, as well as those who depend on one's own work."

Drucker then concludes that, *"In a society in which success has become so terribly important, having options will become increasingly vital."* This is precisely what I have found in developing and applying Simplified Value-Prep® and the COACH Method™: options that previously were hidden are brought to light and have the power to transform the present. So, it is with True Value.

PULLING TOGETHER

No one gets an ironclad guarantee that they get everything they want. Sometimes they get more, much more than they anticipated. At other times, they get most of what they wanted or expected, but not everything. That is the best that can be obtained, given each business' unique circumstances.

My entire business journey has been one of identifying available strengths and resources available—intellectual, physical, and spiritual, and putting that entire base of resources into client service as an advisor. The personal quality of integrity in business has untapped potential to provide answers and guidance for us. *The bottom line is that business as a human activity is most effective when one puts their entire humanity into the work.* My clients and I have witnessed remarkable changes that occur in businesses that should have and would have otherwise failed. Applying systems and processes have resulted in remarkable changes for the better for the betterment of my clients.

Many owners feel stuck or in crisis because they want to do everything themselves. They may be embarrassed or afraid of asking for help because they are hardest on themselves. What they have learned is to *push* themselves harder and harder. Why do we push so hard when that effort sacrifices the very quality of life we are striving to earn?

What do we teach new advisors? The answers are industry compliance, critical thinking, following process, data mining, and data analysis. It is true that these skills are a part of the answer to performance improvements and change relies on those metrics and visible measures. However, it is of equal value to know the practice of questioning and listening, pulling the unseen potentialities from a situation. Those resources which may not be apparent from purely analytics and reasoning are also at our disposal if we are aware of them and know how to apply them. That is the magic and art of transition and transformation. It is getting themes to talk to us and give us the right message as we drill down the data to confirm our insights.

There is immense value in having a deeper understanding of how to develop viable solutions in business, rather than figuring out how to beat the system, numbers or process. Rote answers and short memories tend to repeat failures. In today's age of complexity, we can no longer afford the easy answers. But do not discount the power of simplicity! There are simple solutions which we have overlooked because we are mired in controlling the uncontrollable, like "rolling wire."

When things actually do go haywire, we do not know what to do. That is exactly why a system like Simplified Value-Prep® and the COACH Method™ are invaluable to an owner. There is much more to know and understand than any one of us can manage individually. We at times are forced to drink from the fire hose of information thrown at us each day. We need a stake in the ground to call our own. I believe that stake in business is true value and we must all pursue it together.

THE CHALLENGES FORWARD

We see strategic opportunities all around us. They are present in Renewing to revitalize, Building for growth, Buying for expansion or Selling to exit a business. Today the demands of change are great. Going it alone in business without some form of business value advice can be costly. It is also unrealistic to ignore value with the complexities of business we face every day. There is no need for a client business owner to suffer value-compromising situations in isolation when so many options abound. It is just a matter of finding the right path that makes the most sense in pursuing. It is there. Our mission as Value Advisors is to help find it.

I see value-prepping a business as the significant, competitive differentiator. In the process of applying Simplified Value-Prep® and its COACH Method™, there is an opportunity for making breakthroughs in creative problem-solving and innovation by looking at the business through the lens of true value. By educating others, we can better identify and work through the unseen problems of business that are blockages of progress. I see when a business owner understands value, it takes off unnecessary tension and pressure due to worry. The commitment to finding and building true value transforms energy to pursue strategic objectives to RENEW, BUILD, BUY or SELL with confidence, vigor and passion.

I expect our individual careers will be longer than any generation before us. I also expect we will be in better health to work longer, in a large part to scientific advances and healthcare technology. There is a $10 trillion challenge of business succession over the next 10 years as boomer owners turn over their businesses to the next generation. For the six million privately held businesses and those with employees, I envision a higher quality of business life, which better handles downside risks and uncaps upside potentials. True value insight is where business owners, great individual achievers and great organizations find their touchstone. **A business that has its strength in people, stepping confidently on the path of growth as strategies are seamlessly and flawlessly executed, is unstoppable.**

IT IS TIME TO ADVISE

Timing may or may not be in your client's favor when it is time to sell or transfer their business. We do not have a crystal ball, nor can we predict the events leading up to a sale, those that may influence a renewal effort, a buildout, an acquisition to expand, or a sale to exit. However, we can be prepared for the transfer of true value that we know with 100% certainty happens with every business. Value-prepping is something we do control. There is no better time than now to introduce your business owner clients to the value-prepping process.

The key to being able to take advantage of opportunities confronting the business, or to avoid a catastrophe from a crisis, is to make timing irrelevant. Simplified Value-Prep® puts your business owner client squarely in control. They may be faced with a sudden strategic acquisition opportunity and know there is plenty of cash available to do so, or that they are bankable to get the deal done. There may be a new product line that demands an initial slug of capital or research and development costs to bring it to commercialization, which catapults your client past competitors. Your client may be approached with an opportunity to re-capitalize at a high multiple and take some equity off the table. Whatever situation your client faces in business, value-prepping provides them a critical decision support tool to make the right, creative, and critical decisions.

This is the case for using Simplified Value Prep® and its COACH Method™. That is why every business owner needs to consider and answer the question now: to Value-Prep, or not to Value-Prep? I assure you, that answer is the single most influential and important business decision your clients will ever make. It is my hope you will join me in introducing this concept of true value to your current and new clients.

Make it EASY,

David Wayne Wimer, Founder
www.value-prep.com

VALUE CONCEPTS &
FINANCIAL DEFINITIONS

"Business Value Preparation" is an organizational strategy that emphasizes actions designed to prepare the business and owner to be and remain in a constant 'readiness state,' so that at any time, for any purpose, value is optimized, regardless of chance or choice events. Actions underpin a proven process for being organized and prepared, and therefore in a constant 'ready' state, regardless of chance or choice events that may occur, thereby protecting business value.

"Certified Business Intermediary" (CBI®) is an experienced business broker who is committed to the highest level of professional development the industry has to offer and has ethical values aligned with the IBBA® standards of professionalism. A CBI® can objectively guide clients through the intricacies of the entire marketing and negotiation process of a business sale, resulting in successful transactions and satisfied clients. Along with having undergone a specialized initial program of detailed training, a CBI is required to earn continuing education credits to maintain the credential.

"Certified Financial Planner" (CFP™) certification is the standard of excellence in financial planning. CFP® professionals meet rigorous education, training, and ethical standards, and are committed to serving their clients' best interests today to prepare them for a more secure tomorrow. They use their knowledge and expertise to construct personalized financial plans that aim to achieve the financial goals of clients. These plans include not only investments but also savings, budget, insurance, and tax strategies.

"Certified Valuation Analyst" (CVA®) is established by the National Association of Certified Valuators and Analysts® (NACVA®), and it is the only valuation credential accredited by the National Commission for Certifying Agencies® (NCCA®), the accreditation body of the Institute for Credentialing Excellence™ (ICE™), and the American National Standards Institute® (ANSI®). The CVA designation is an indication to the business, professional, and legal communities that recipients have met the rigorous standards of professionalism, expertise, objectivity, and integrity in the field of business valuation, financial consulting and litigation, and related consulting disciplines.

"Case-based Learning" is an essential part of business education as it enables students to discover and develop their unique framework for dealing with business problems, using an actual Case Study. The important peculiarity of the business case study is that it introduces a slice of realism into the learning experience. The case study method helps the students in developing wisdom and broadens the scope for knowledge application on a live situation they may encounter in the market.

"Case Study" is the most effective teaching technique of practical application skills in today's business environment. It enables students examining different business situations, in various cultural and economic perspectives, to open their minds by navigating a genuine business situation.

"COACH" is an acronym for the four actions of Business Value Preparation in the COACH Method™ :
I.Calculate – an Enterprise Value
II.Orient – to the goals & objectives of the owner
III.Adapt – make changes to support goals & objectives
IV.CHoose – evaluate new options

"COACH Method™" is the step-by-step process methodology for Business Value Preparation using the four actions to achieve a constant state of business readiness, prepared for any reason, including chance or choice events.

"COACH Quadrant" is one of the four Action Quadrants in the COACH Method™. The Quadrants are: Calculate. Orient. Adapt. CHoose.

"Cross-Functional Teams" are a short-term group of people from different areas of the business who come together for specific problem-solving or continuous improvement. Usually, the team is put in place for rapid change management inside the business with specific objectives to accomplish. The group has a leader and a communications path direct to the owner. Team characteristics also include diversity, collaboration, excellent communications skills, the authority to make decisions, and a process-orientation.

"EBITDA" is Earnings Before Interest, Taxes, Depreciation & Amortization, and is used in calculating business value. Average EBITDA is the mean of computing several years and dividing by the number of years. Weighted EBITDA is the weighting of more recent years higher than earlier years, giving the benefit of more recent performance to the business value.

"Enterprise Value" (EV) is a measure of a company's total value, often used as a more comprehensive alternative to equity market capitalization. Enterprise value includes in its calculation the market capitalization of a company, but also short-term and long-term debt, as well as any cash on the company's balance sheet.

"Fair Market Value" (FMV) in its simplest sense, is the price an asset would sell for on the open market. FMV has come to represent the price of an asset under the following usual set of conditions: prospective buyers and sellers are knowledgeable about the asset, behaving in their own best interest, free of undue pressure to trade, and given a reasonable time for completing the transaction. Given these conditions, an asset's FMV should represent an accurate valuation or assessment of its worth.

"Family Office" provides a broad spectrum of private wealth management services to one or a small number of ultra-high-net-worth families. Besides financial services, family offices also offer planning, charitable giving advice, concierge, and other comprehensive services. Single-family offices serve one individual and their family, while multi-family offices serve a few families benefiting from economies of scale.

"FINRA" means the Financial Industry Regulatory Authority, Inc.; (a) "FINRA Board" means the FINRA Board of Governors; (b) "FINRA member" means any broker or dealer admitted to membership in FINRA.

"FINRA Series" administered by FINRA and known as the general securities representative license. The Series 7 license authorizes an agent to sell virtually any type of individual security, such as preferred stocks, options, bonds, and other individual fixed income investments—plus all forms of packaged products.

"Financial Advisor" is a professional who provides expertise for an individual's decisions around money matters, personal finances, and investments called a Personal Financial Plan.

Financial advisors may work as independent agents, or they may be employed by a larger financial firm. They are FINRA licensed for the representation of any type of individual security. Also known as Registered Financial Advisors. Unlike stockbrokers, who simply execute orders in the market, registered financial advisors provide guidance and make informed decisions on behalf of their clients.

"Merger & Acquisition Master Intermediary" (M&AMI®)
The M&A Source® Merger & Acquisition Master Intermediary® Certification is a proprietary designation that affords professional growth and marketability unlike any other in the M&A profession. This title distinguishes each of the holders as seasoned M&A professionals who have a solid educational background, proven accomplishments in completing deals, and a strong passion for the M&A Source and the M&A profession. The Master designation is the only one to require both educational credits and the successful completion of multiple middle-market transactions.

"Owner's Wish List" is a document that outlines the business owner's goals and objectives during the Orient Quadrant of the COACH Method™ for Simplified Value-Prep. It addresses what the owner wants from the business long-term. During a negotiation it would address what the owner sees as key deal points to accomplish. Having a written, numbered list assists the owner in clarifying wants and needs and prioritizes the efforts of the lead negotiator.

"Letter of Guidance" is the list of critical items an owner creates in case of emergency (ICE) should the owner be incapacitated. The one-page document includes key professionals such as CPA, Attorney and Advisors of the business, who may be left in charge of the business in the interim period or who may be the family member liaison, a list of passwords and bank accounts which can be referenced to a secure electronic vault, and any specific items that may only be known quickly by an owner.

"Multiple" is applied to a specific financial metric of a company to calculate the business' valuation or assess its reasonability. The most common financial metrics that multiples are applied to include EBITDA, EBIT, Net Earnings, and Revenue. If a multiple is applied to a pre-debt number, like EBITDA, EBIT or Revenue, the resulting valuation is the estimated enterprise value. If the multiple is applied to an after-debt number, such as net earnings, the resulting valuation is the estimated equity value. A multiple is referred to as "4 times", "4x" or "4 turns", as an example, which would refer to EBITDA being multiplied times four to yield the estimated valuation of a company.

"Opportunity Analysis" is the list of potential changes in the business to close Value Gaps. Each Opportunity is defined on a spreadsheet by a description of the goal, project leader, team members, and action(s) to be taken, prioritized by the financial return to the business. An owner, sponsoring change, may use the Opportunity Analysis to attack low-hanging fruit, to achieve easy wins building confidence of the cross-collaborative team. Owner(s) can track and measure progress over short, 90-day windows when initiating change.

"Pareto Principle of 80/20" is named after Vilfredo Pareto who in 1906 at the age of fifty-eight observed that 20% of the population owned 80% of the land in Italy. Pareto was an Italian civil engineer, sociologist, economist, political scientist, and philosopher. The 80-20 rule, also known as the Pareto Principle, is an aphorism which asserts that 80% of outcomes (or outputs) result from 20% of all causes (or inputs) for any given event. In the context of value improvement, Pareto is applied as a prioritization tool given that resources are finite when making changes in the business. In other words, Pareto gets "more bang for the buck."

"Personal Financial Plan" is a modeling tool designed for managing personal finances. It encompasses budgeting, banking, insurance, mortgages, investments, retirement planning, and tax and estate planning. The model uses current income and expenses at any one point in time to project future needs compared to the needs and desires of the individual or household. The plan includes certain agreed upon assumptions of inflation and growth and the appreciation of assets. The plan is effective as a decision support tool for meeting financial goals, such as income, spending, and overall investing strategies.

"Professional Advisors" in the context of a business, is a professional who assists the owner of a business with specific expertise. Advisors are external professionals such as a CPA, Tax CPA, Business Attorney, Tax Attorney, Patent Attorney, Litigation Attorney, Certified Valuation Analyst, Certified Financial Planner, Wealth Advisor, Value Advisor, M&A Advisor, or any other subject-matter expert utilized as a consultant to the business owner.

"Readiness State" in the context of Business Value Preparation & Protection means: At any time, for any reason, the business can be transferred for maximum value, regardless of choice or chance events.

"Simplified Value-Prep®" (SVP®) is the registered service mark for the design of the COACH Method™, a process for Business Value Preparation & Protection. Business brokers & M&A advisors utilize SVP to prepare a business for sale or transfer and maximize its value.

"Valuation" is a calculation that depends upon purpose and is used to determine a range of Fair Market Value for any business.

"Value" is short for Fair Market Value, the price at which a business would sell given the financial and operating condition of the business at that point in time, under the conditions of Fair Market Value.

"Value Advisor" is a person skilled in understanding FMV Valuations for the purposes of business planning, value preparation, and protection. They may or may not be certified as a Valuation Analyst. The Value Advisor usually depends upon their experience and knowledge of markets. The Value Advisor may also be known as a Corporate Financial Advisor who works with business owners to understand the big picture of Balance Sheet and Profit & Loss reports, Forecasting, Operating Budgets and Financing strategies employed in the business.

"Value Factors Assessment" is a self-assessment with 50+ factors that are rated by the owner to view the business in terms of Value, which leads to discussions of Value Gaps.

"Value Gap Analysis" is the identification of any gap between a) what an owner may perceive as Value, b) what a Fair Market Value (FMV) Valuation is for the business, and c) what the current market may indicate through comparable sales and industry reports, taking into consideration economic climate.

"Value Mindset" is a view on using value in the business as a key performance indicator and standard business tool. It includes teaching value concepts to people in the business who understand drivers of value and detractors of value. Everyone becomes oriented to a value mindset, growth and risk mitigation in the business.

"Value-Prep Plan" is the outcome of using the Simplified Value-Prep® process for business value preparation and protection. The Value-Prep Plan is managed on Value-Prep.com, a cloud-based, on-line electronic vault to track, store and organize electronic documents. The Value-Prep Plan is confidential, cyber-secure, and meets the requirements of critical privacy standards such as HIPAA & CCPA.

"Value-Prepping" is the act of using Simplified Value-Prep®.

"Wealth Management Advisor" is a high-level professional who manages an affluent client's wealth holistically, typically for one set fee. This service is usually appropriate for wealthy individuals with a broad array of diverse needs.

THE SIMPLIFIED VALUE-PREP® MODEL

The COACH Method™ underpins a proven process for Value-Prepping a business to be in a constant 'readiness' state, regardless of chance or choice events that may occur, thereby protecting business value. More can be learned at Value-Prep.com.

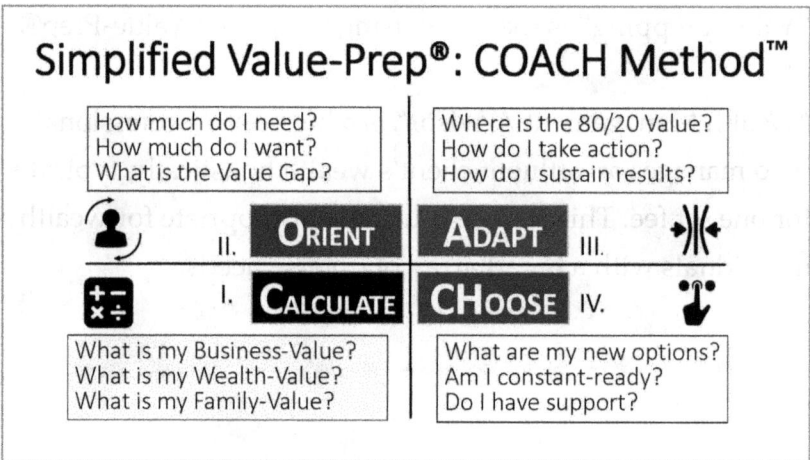

Simplified Value-Prep®: COACH Method™

How much do I need?
How much do I want?
What is the Value Gap?

Where is the 80/20 Value?
How do I take action?
How do I sustain results?

II. ORIENT — ADAPT III.

I. CALCULATE — CHOOSE IV.

What is my Business-Value?
What is my Wealth-Value?
What is my Family-Value?

What are my new options?
Am I constant-ready?
Do I have support?

LIKED THE ADVISOR'S GUIDE?

Check out The Tale of Mac and Murphy: The Most Important Business Decision You'll Ever Make

If you enjoyed *The Advisor's Guide,* please consider leaving an unbiased review on Amazon, Audible, Goodreads or Bookbub to help spread the word. You can learn more about this book and the author at
https://davidwimer.com/

Contact or follow the author at
Contact: davidwimer.com/contact

www.ingramcontent.com/pod-product-compliance
Lightning Source LLC
Chambersburg PA
CBHW071702210326
41597CB00017B/2287